Improving Adolescent Literacy

An RTI Implementation Guide

Pamela S. Craig, Ph.D., and
Rebecca K. Sarlo, Ph.D.

Eye On Education
6 Depot Way West, Suite 106
Larchmont, NY 10538
(914) 833-0551
(914) 833-0761 fax
www.eyeoneducation.com

Library of Congress Cataloging-in-Publication Data

Craig, Pamela S.
Improving adolescent literacy: an RTI implementation guide / by Pamela
S. Craig and Rebecca Sarlo.
     p.   cm.
ISBN 978-1-59667-204-8
1. Reading (Secondary)
2. Response to intervention (Learning disabled children)
I. Sarlo, Rebecca.
II. Title.
LB1632.C73 2011
428.4071′2--dc23   2011038305

10 9 8 7 6 5 4 3 2 1

Sponsoring Editor: Robert Sickles
Production Editor: Lauren Davis
Copyeditor: Dorothy Anderson
Designer and Compositor: Matthew Williams, click! Publishing Services
Cover Designer: Dave Strauss, 3FoldDesign

Also Available from EYE ON EDUCATION

About the Authors

Dr. Pamela Craig, author of *Literacy Leadership Teams: Collaborative Leadership for Improving and Sustaining Student Achievement*, has spent the past eight years as a literacy specialist working with low-performing schools throughout the state of Florida. She currently serves as a Regional Executive Director for the Florida Department of Education providing support to improve student achievement at low performing schools. She taught high school language arts for 11 years and has presented at state and national conferences on a myriad of topics focusing on instructional practices related to improving adolescent literacy. She earned her Ph.D. in Curriculum and Instruction from the University of South Florida in 2006. She was named the Florida Council of Teachers of English (FCTE) 2001 Teacher of the Year and currently serves as the President for FCTE. She resides in Bradenton, Florida, with her husband, three children, and five grandchildren.

Dr. Rebecca Sarlo has devoted her career to serving struggling schools throughout the state of Florida. She currently serves as the Problem Solving/Response to Intervention (PS/RTI) Secondary School Coordinator for Florida's PS/RTI Project. Within this position, she is responsible for the development of a state-wide secondary RTI model and for supporting schools and districts to utilize PS/RTI to meet the needs of all students. Previously, Dr. Sarlo was employed by the Florida Department of Education, where she served on a regional accountability and support team as the RTI Specialist. She began her career as a school psychologist, enjoying this work for nine years. She earned her Ph.D. in School Psychology from the University of South Florida and is a nationally certified school psychologist. Dr. Sarlo has taught undergraduate and graduate level education courses focused on instructional design, child development and learning, and effective communication and consultation. She presents at numerous state and national conferences on topics ranging from school improvement to strategic planning, prevention and early intervention, formative assessment, and student engagement. She resides in Clearwater, Florida, with her two children, Madelyn and Ashton, who remind her every day why her work is so important.

Acknowledgments

No author can write without the support of family and friends who put up with our absence at events and mood swings when writing hits the wall. I am no exception. I am indebted to my family and friends who encourage me to continue to put into words the passions that fill my days. I am especially appreciative of my husband, Randy, who supports my endeavors even when it means that I am preoccupied.

I am also grateful for the incredible collegial relationships that guide my thinking and force me to look beyond the obvious. I sincerely appreciate those who challenge me to think about my work and to delve deeper for the answers. Thank you to Gina, who reminds me to keep it simple; to Matt, who challenges my thinking; to Mason, who questions everything; and to Mike, who always brings me back to focusing on the people we impact.

In our work with schools, we are continuously amazed by the expertise that exists in every school and district. Often our only task is to make obvious to the school team the answers they already have. Through these relationships, I have come to understand that sustainable school change that positively impacts students' ability to learn is achievable when we work together as a team. It is that hope that forces me to continue my professional journey.

Finally, I am appreciative of my work with Rebecca, who gave me the terminology to explain my vision. It is the culmination of our work together that leads to sustainable change in the schools we visit.

—Pam

There are so many important people in my life who made this book possible and who deserve special thanks and recognition. First and foremost, I would like to thank my children, Madelyn and Ashton, who not only were patient and understanding regarding the many hours I spent engaged in the writing process but also provide me with inspiration every day to do my part in improving the educational experiences of Florida's public school students.

I would also like to thank the multitude of friends and family members who helped and supported me on a moment's notice. Although there are too many individuals to thank herein, I do wish to specifically thank my sister Angela Garza, my friend and neighbor Beth Heintz, and my mother- and father-in-law, Alan and Nancy Sarlo, who supplied endless hours of playtime for my children and words of encouragement for me. In addition to these friends and family, I offer a special thank-you to my dear friend Bob Lynch, whose unwavering confidence in my ability to balance the demands of a challenging career while raising two children and writing a book encouraged me to continue moving forward, even when I felt in over my head.

My greatest source of inspiration for writing this book and for my work in general came from my late father, Charles Finkler. My father taught me from an early age the importance of hard work and spoke often of the power of public service. He was most proud of my work with and for children, and although he passed away during the writing of this book, I know that he would have brimmed with pride upon its completion.

I am incredibly thankful for the amazing opportunity to work with and learn from educators serving Florida's most struggling schools. I am often in awe of the commitment that these individuals demonstrate and am thankful for their devotion to our future. The experiences I have shared with Pam have been especially transformative. Teaming with such a knowledgeable and committed professional has prompted immense professional growth of which I am both proud and thankful.

—Rebecca

Table of Contents

Foreword

I have spent my entire career figuring out ways that schools can respond to the increasing literacy demands on adolescents. Over the years, I have worked with content teachers to help them integrate literacy support into rigorous content learning. The last decade of my work, however, has been the most exciting because I have been able to help middle and high school literacy leaders develop, implement, and monitor school-wide systems, schedules, and action plans to improve literacy and learning for all students. School and district literacy leaders often reel when they consider Common Core State Standards, response to intervention, and various levels of state accountability systems. These requirements, though, all have the same goal—to improve the level of literacy and learning for students. Taking the viewpoint of literacy as a school-wide issue is essential to improve schools. Each school and district must figure out the best way to approach a literacy improvement effort within the context of the students and community they serve. It is this school-wide view of improving literacy that makes this book a strong contribution to the field of adolescent literacy.

Response to intervention has helped educators at all levels of schooling rethink how to serve the literacy needs of all students. The authors' previous work with literacy teams in middle and high schools serves as a solid foundation for taking a problem-solving approach to decision making. *Improving Adolescent Literacy* is full of practical approaches, useful information, and guiding questions that will help literacy leaders. This book helps middle and high school literacy leaders understand the components of RTI and develop instruction so that all students can develop the literacy proficiency they need to succeed in school, at the workplace, and as citizens. I know many school and district leaders will find this book a helpful resource as they work to make their schools responsive to the literacy needs of students.

—Dr. Judith L. Irvin, Professor
Florida State University

1

Adolescent Literacy

An effective reading program develops reading competence in all students and is based on proven practices. Three components are critical to the design, implementation, and sustainability of powerful reading instruction: professional development that equips educators with a solid knowledge base; effective instructional tools that are aligned to the knowledge base; and school systems that support and nurture implementation.

—Diamond, 2006

Improving students' ability to read and comprehend increasingly complex texts across grade levels and content areas is the foundation for all effective school-reform initiatives. The vast amount of information students are now required to absorb and synthesize into working knowledge requires today's youth to develop complex literacy skills not required of students in the past. As a result, teachers are being asked to move away from the conventional lecture model, which exposes students to the essential details most likely to appear on a test, and toward facilitating students' active participation in the learning process. This shift is critical if the goal is to enable students to continue to access, absorb, and synthesize new information as they move into adulthood. Thus, educators must shift from the traditional instructional model that focuses on teaching students what to think about by providing a "trivial pursuit" of facts and details toward a more complex system of teaching students how to think.

Changing tradition is not an easy task. However, when we begin to examine state and national standards, it becomes clear that how we measure student achievement is changing and with that change must come modifications to instruction. Many states are moving toward educator evaluation systems that evaluate teachers not on what is covered but instead on what students learn. This means that teachers can no longer close their doors and continue to deliver instruction independent of the school-wide literacy goals but instead must work collaboratively with their peers to develop instructional plans and systems that address the needs of all students.

Shifting from covering the content to teaching students how to be active, independent learners requires educators to adopt a new way of thinking about adolescent literacy. It will also require that teachers adopt a new way of work, making the most of their collective capacity to meet their students' needs and maximize student literacy outcomes. It has been our experience that teams that adopt a problem-solving/response to intervention (PS/RTI) framework as a means of developing common instructional goals for all students, identifying barriers to student learning, designing and implementing instructional plans to address the barriers, and consistently and regularly monitoring student progress are more successful in achieving their school literacy goals than schools that do not adopt such a framework. As such, we hope to provide readers with practical recommendations and research-based resources to begin to better address their students' literacy needs through the implementation of a PS/RTI framework in their schools. Ultimately, our goal is that with the guidance and resources provided herein, literacy leadership teams will take the first step toward better understanding their students' needs and making the changes necessary to ensure their students' success.

Defining Literacy

Traditionally, literacy is defined as the ability to read and write. However, determining whether or not a student possesses sufficient reading and writing skills is not that simple. It is, in fact, sometimes controversial. Most high school teachers can share examples of students who can read words and write legibly but who can't effectively read grade-level text with comprehension on their own. Some adults possess the ability to read simple language and are capable of holding jobs but have difficulty reading more complex texts, such as journal articles, informational texts, loan papers, or contractual agreements. Others are capable of reading more complex texts if they are relevant to their daily lives but spend little time reading for pleasure or gathering information outside their immediate needs. Still others possess the skills to read a variety of texts for a variety of purposes and apply those skills on a regular basis. In essence, people possess various levels of literacy, ranging from those with very limited literacy skills to those who exhibit highly complex literacy skills. Educators are left to answer the question, "What constitutes 'sufficient' literacy skills?"

To begin to answer this question, we turn to the UNESCO Institute for Education (2008), which defines literacy as:

> the ability to identify, understand, interpret, create, communicate and compute using printed and written materials associated with varying contexts. Literacy involves a continuum of learning in enabling [an individual] to achieve his or her goals, develop his or her knowledge and potentials, and participate fully in the community and wider society. (p. 25)

This definition provides a detailed explanation of what one should consider "sufficient" literacy skills. Clearly, the definition goes far beyond simply decoding words or recalling facts. Instead, a student's ability to read increasingly complex texts, requiring increasingly complex literacy skills, has become the gatekeeper not only to higher education but also to the ability to function and prosper within society as well as in the global marketplace. As a result, we argue the role of education is to ensure that students possess the skills necessary to allow them to function as literate adults, fully capable of participating in and adapting to an ever-changing society. For this to occur, schools that serve students in grades 4 through 12 must begin the process of redefining curriculum and instruction in order to incorporate literacy support as part of daily instruction across all content areas.

Literacy as a School-Wide Issue

The implementation of the No Child Left Behind Act of 2001 focused on reading in grades K through 3 while essentially ignoring the importance of reinforcing reading/literacy skills beyond grade 3. Unfortunately, it is not unusual to discover that students who perform well on reading assessments in grade 3 often struggle on subsequent reading assessments. The acquisition of skills required for students to read with comprehension become more difficult over time because texts become increasingly complex, focus on highly complex topics and themes, contain information in multiple formats, and require students to synthesize information from a variety of sources and formats (Carnegie Council on Advancing Adolescent Literacy, 2010). Students in grades 4 through 12 are often expected to read increasingly complex texts independently without the benefit of instructional support. Lacking continued literacy instruction and support, once-proficient students begin to fall behind, becoming more dependent on teachers to provide them with information from text rather than developing the skills necessary to read independently and gather their own information. Over time, students' lack of literacy skills are compounded by a decrease in the time students spend reading, which negatively impacts their achievement across all content areas. As a result, we begin with the belief that literacy should be regarded as a system-wide issue, requiring both a school-wide and a vertical articulation response from schools that serve students in grades 4 through 12.

The call to provide continued reading support and development for students in grades 4 through 12 is reinforced through substantial research on adolescent literacy (Carnegie Council on Advancing Adolescent Literacy, 2010; Fang & Schleppegrell, 2010; Moje, 2008; Shanahan & Shanahan, 2008; Heller & Greenleaf, 2007; National Institute for Literacy, 2007; Meltzer, Smith, & Clark, 2002). Despite substantial evidence to the contrary, many secondary schools approach adolescent literacy with the belief that once students receive the foundational reading instruction provided in grades K through 3, they no longer require additional reading instruction. Snow and Moje (2010) refer to this misconception as the "inoculation fallacy" and contend that simply providing students with foundational reading instruction is insufficient to support student achievement over time and, ultimately, will not allow educators to adequately contend with the adolescent literacy crisis we now face.

A New Approach to Adolescent Literacy

Instead of falling victim to the inoculation fallacy, school systems must begin to build and implement effective literacy programming beginning in grade 4 and continuing through grade 12. The intensity of adolescent literacy issues demands that these literacy initiatives include both high-quality literacy instruction across core academic areas to support all students' comprehension of increasingly complex text combined with targeted remediation for students whose reading skills are below grade level. The long-term success of literacy programs and ultimately successful school reform are accomplished through effective literacy programs that address the needs of all learners rather than focusing only on students who are not meeting grade-level standards. Thus, we warn schools that developing reading intervention programs without ensuring the existence of high-quality core instruction is unlikely to achieve the desired student outcomes.

The adoption of a PS/RTI framework will assist schools to identify and define specific literacy problems, ascertain and analyze the barriers to improving student literacy outcomes, develop and implement a research-based literacy program, and monitor progress toward achieving desired goals in order to determine the effectiveness of the plan.

The implementation of a PS/RTI framework will allow teams to develop effective literacy programing that includes the following:

- ◆ A multitiered system of student supports
  - Cross-curricular reading comprehension strategy instruction
  - Targeted reading intervention for students reading below grade level
- ◆ Data-based problem solving
  - Identification of barriers to improved student literacy outcomes
  - Design of instructional/intervention programming to address identified barriers
  - Progress monitoring to determine effectiveness of instruction and intervention plans
- ◆ Teacher support through professional development and instructional coaching

Multitiered System of Student Supports

The implementation of a multitiered system of student supports serves as the basis for a comprehensive literacy program. Providing multitiered supports ensures that all students have access to the intensity of instruction required to support their progress toward grade-level literacy goals. Within a multi-tiered system, all students receive "core" instruction, the focus and intensity (e.g., amount of time) of which is determined through an analysis of school-wide data. Some students may require an intensification of core instruction, which can be accomplished through differentiation designed to address individual student literacy needs. Differentiation within core instruction may be sufficient to meet the needs of some students, while others may continue to require more intensive supports. Determining the intensity of student needs is best accomplished through the ongoing collection and analysis of progress-monitoring data (Carnegie Council on Advancing Adolescent Literacy, 2010; Gutierrez, 2009; Wise, 2009). Students whose progress is insufficient to meet literacy goals with core instruction and differentiation may require supplemental literacy support in addition to core instruction.

However, schools that find a substantial percentage of their students reading below grade level and/or making insufficient progress toward literacy goals should consider strategies to strengthen core literacy instruction school-wide as the first line of defense. Moving away from an intervention model to an intial instruction model requires a significant shift in thinking at the secondary level. With this shift, literacy instruction becomes an integral part of core instruction and is embedded across the curriculum to ensure all students are developing the skills they need to independently comprehend increasingly complex texts across disciplines and grade levels.

In addition to strengthening core instruction, schools should consider scheduling reading intervention time within their master schedule to allow for additional supplemental literacy instruction. With time built into the master schedule, students who are not demonstrating progress within core instruction alone have ready access to additional support and instruction (i.e., Tier 2 and Tier 3 intervention) (Brozo, 2010).

Core Literacy Instruction (Tier 1). The importance of core literacy instruction is never more evident than when a school's instructional teams identify barriers to students' success within their specific content areas. Without fail, regardless of the content area, student literacy issues are typically identified as the primary barrier to students' success, highlighting literacy as a school-wide issue.

Designing effective core literacy instruction begins with reviewing student literacy data to determine the percentage of students with grade-level literacy skills. A school that determines that fewer than 80% to 85% of its students are reading on grade level should begin by focusing on strengthening core literacy instruction. Schools with more than 85% of their students demonstrating reading proficiency may conclude that core instruction is adequate for addressing the needs of the majority of the students and is, therefore, effective. In this case, the school may choose to focus on developing tiered intervention supports to address the needs of the 15% to 20% of students for whom the core is not sufficient. Unfortunately, it has been our experience that a majority of secondary schools face percentages of nonproficient students well beyond 15% to 20% and must, therefore, focus on core instructional planning.

Once the percentage of proficient students has been determined, the next step is to set reasonable yet ambitious school-wide student literacy goals. For example, a school may set a goal to increase the percentage of proficient readers from 65% to 70% by the end of the school year. However, just determining a literacy goal is not sufficient to ensure improving student literacy outcomes. Teachers will need support to understand how improvements in literacy will translate into improved student outcomes within their own classrooms. Otherwise, many will view this goal as irrelevant to their own teaching. As such, schools must include within their plans sufficient teacher support to ensure teacher buy-in. Thus, part of a well-defined plan must focus on teacher professional development and support to unite the staff around the literacy goal.

After establishing and building consensus around literacy goals, the next step entails working collaboratively with instructional personnel to identify barriers that have precluded or could prevent the school from achieving the literacy goals. These barriers serve as the basis for the development of a school-wide literacy program that is implemented in every classroom across the school.

Core instruction serves as the foundation for all additional instruction. Supplemental (Tier 2 and Tier 3) intervention is provided in addition to core instruction for those students whose needs cannot be met through core instruction alone. Supplemental instruction is not meant to replace core instruction but is designed to provide additional support above and beyond core instruction in order to enhance the likelihood that students will be successful within their core courses (Brozo, 2010).

For many secondary teachers, the idea of setting literacy goals and including literacy instruction as part of content area instruction may seem foreign. Some teachers may complain that students in middle and high school should have already been taught how to read and that taking time during content-specific instruction to devote to teaching students to read undermines their curriculum. These same teachers often recognize many of their students cannot comprehend the assigned text, so they devote countless hours creating PowerPoint presentations, developing and sharing Cornell Notes on the overhead, or simply handing their students outlines of the text in student-friendly language in hopes that students will learn the material presented. This approach allows teachers to "cover" the curriculum but is not particularly effective in helping students develop the highly complex skills they need to access content on their own. The result is that students' ability to become self-sufficient, independent learners is severely limited because students never develop the literacy skills they need.

Accordingly, a majority of secondary school teachers will benefit from support to understand how to help students develop "disciplinary literacy" skills required within their content areas (Moje, 2008; Shanahan & Shanahan, 2008). The concept surrounding disciplinary literacy requires that educators examine what it means to *learn* the content as opposed to simply *know* the content. This shift from *knowing* to *learning* requires that students develop a set of advanced literacy skills that allows them access to complex text across content areas. These advanced literacy skills do not simply develop as a result of foundational reading instruction. Instead, they require teachers to provide students with literacy strategies that students can employ when meaning breaks down, improving the students' abilities to think critically, solve complex problems, and generalize knowledge beyond the educational setting. When teachers begin to examine what skills are necessary for students to *learn* within their content classes rather than simply be able to *know* or recall information, they are more apt to shift their focus away from telling students what they need to know toward helping students develop the skills they need to become active, independent learners.

To this end, core literacy instruction ideally includes direct, explicit instruction in reading comprehension and vocabulary acquisition strategies combined with access to diverse texts and multiple opportunities to practice applying the strategies with feedback across texts from various content areas (Carnegie Council on Advancing Adolescent Literacy, 2010; Kamil, Borman, Dole, Kral, Salinger, & Torgensen, 2008). It is important to note that literacy skills that are taught in isolation and are not connected to content area learning are unlikely to be highly effective (Langer, 2001). Literacy instruction and support should be embedded and integrated within core content instruction as a means of supporting student learning and should not be presented as a set of isolated tasks. Connecting literacy instruction to the process of learning content material is essential. Students who understand the connection between literacy skills and strategies and the mastery of content material are typically more motivated to engage in the learning process and apply the literacy skills or strategies within their content classes than are students who experience the literacy instruction as disconnected and unrelated to their content area learning.

For many students, the connection between literacy instruction and content area learning must be explicit. Teaching students to apply concepts and strategies across multiple texts, especially grade-level content area texts and supplemental materials, fosters student understanding of the utility of literacy strategies and skills beyond reading and language arts classrooms (Langer, 2001).

Ultimately, core instruction should be designed with an understanding that students are most likely to become independent, disciplined learners when literacy instruction includes explicit reading and writing instruction with multiple opportunities for students to practice these skills within authentic and relevant reading and writing tasks. Thus, the plans must include provisions to provide all teachers with the support necessary to integrate literacy instruction into students' daily lives.

Reading Intervention Instruction (Tier 2 and Tier 3). Small group and/or individual, personalized literacy interventions provided in addition to core instruction are likely necessary to provide adequate support for students who are reading significantly below grade level. These supplemental tiers of instruction are provided in addition to the core and not in place of core instruction.

Tiered intervention supports are most likely to be effective when they are closely aligned with core instruction, focused on achieving core literacy goals, and scheduled within the school's master schedule. Pull-out programs, which provide literacy instruction during the time when a student is scheduled to receive core instruction, are unlikely to be effective and in most cases result in students falling behind in their core course work. Likewise, invitational intervention programs, such as those that are offered to students before and after school, during lunch, or on Saturdays, are likely to be ineffective due to low attendance rates (Bottoms, 1998). Thus, schools should strive to set aside time within their master schedules to provide literacy intervention. Enrolling students in literacy interventions scheduled into the master schedule is likely to produce much better results than enrolling them in invitational intervention programs.

To maximize literacy intervention results, instruction within reading intervention courses must be provided by skilled literacy specialists and targeted to meet student needs indicated by diagnostic data and information (Carnegie Council on Advancing Adolescent Literacy, 2010; Gutierrez, 2009; Heller & Greenleaf, 2007). Unfortunately, in many schools, teachers assigned to reading intervention classes are beginning teachers with little or no experience and/or training in reading. In order to compensate for teacher inexperience, many schools adopt highly scripted, research-based reading programs in hopes that such programs will overshadow the instruction. However, as Langer (2001) suggests, the skill of the teacher plays a significant role in the effectiveness of the program. For instance, highly effective teachers regularly analyze student assessments and use the results of these assessments to make timely instructional and curricular adjustments. These timely and critical changes to instruction are best made by well-informed, skilled teachers who understand the needs of their students. Highly skilled teachers are more likely than the literacy program publishers to understand the individual needs of their students.

While most research-based reading programs cite data supporting their success, in reality no single program exists that meets the needs of all readers. Therefore, reading intervention teachers must be skilled at identifying the specific remediation needs of their students through analysis of data and at identifying and providing specific reading interventions designed to support those remediation needs (Carnegie Council on Advancing Adolescent Literacy, 2010; Wise, 2009; Heller & Greenleaf, 2007).

The Complexity of Adolescent Literacy Issues

The difficulties surrounding adolescent literacy issues are evident to most secondary-school educators. Given the complexities of the issue, adolescent literacy demands a multidimensional and comprehensive response beyond that required in early elementary school. In the primary grades, students are learning how to read and focusing on decoding and fluency skills. Once students possess basic reading skills or have reached third grade (whichever comes first), the instructional focus begins to change from teaching students how to read toward teaching them how to learn from reading. Some students make this transition seamlessly, while others experience this transition as tenuous and difficult. Regardless of students' ease of transition, we are beginning to understand that most students, including those who have mastered foundational reading skills and transitioned readily from learning to read to reading to learn, continue to require instruction and support to meet ever-increasing text demands (Jacobs, 2008).

As students move into the intermediate grades, they begin to deal with a myriad of factors influencing their ability and motivation to learn. Students' reading proficiency is impacted by the increasing demands of texts (e.g., longer texts; increased word, sentence, and structural complexity; inclusion of graphic representations; and varying text structures across disciplines) combined with changes in student social-emotional development (e.g., developing sense of identity, increasing need for independence and autonomy, and competing priorities involving peers, family, and work), all of which influence their motivation to engage in learning activities (Carnegie Council on Advancing Adolescent Literacy, 2010; Kamil et al., 2008; Moje, Overby, Tysvaer, & Morris, 2008). Students who lack reading skills and who disengage from school in general or from reading in particular are not likely to acquire grade-level reading skills and are significantly at risk for accruing content course failures and eventually dropping out of school (Hammond, Linton, Smink, & Drew, 2007). Thus, literacy plans and programs must be designed to address not only the literacy needs of students but also student engagement issues through a careful consideration of students' evolving social-emotional needs.

Diagnostic Assessment Data

Schools that use disaggregated diagnostic data in addition to state-mandated summative assessment data as a resource for providing more targeted instruction are more successful at closing the achievement gap for all students than those that do not (Oberman & Symonds, 2005). Having said that, we urge schools to recognize that student achievement is influenced by multiple factors beyond student skill development and profile, including students' access to high-quality curriculum and instruction, student motivation and engagement, teacher preparation, and school culture. "Diagnosing" and intervening effectively with adolescent literacy issues will likely require school teams to consider each of these variables.

Progress Monitoring

As reiterated throughout this chapter, progress monitoring of student achievement is paramount to the success of any literacy action plan. Data is required not only to develop the plan but also to modify the plan over time (Carnegie Council on Advancing Adolescent Literacy, 2010). Assessments should be selected or designed to allow the school to consistently answer the question, "Are our literacy programs sufficient to meet the needs of our students and to meet our literacy goals?" Without collecting and analyzing student literacy data over time, educators are forced to guess which, if any, instructional changes are needed and to simply hope, rather than know, that the benefits of providing the existing literacy programming are worth the cost.

With that said, we caution schools about the danger of placing too much emphasis on the collection of assessment data and not enough emphasis on interpreting the data in order to make sound instructional decisions. Simply having data will not result in more successful literacy programming unless teachers possess the skills and supports necessary to make instructional decisions based on systematic data analysis. We have found that while the majority of schools have access to multiple data sources, most schools underuse their data to inform their decision making. Ensuring teachers are provided time to fully understand and analyze the data in order to make informed curricular and instructional decisions requires careful planning by administrators. Ignoring these elements results in teacher and student frustration at seemingly useless testing routines and yields few results in significant changes in student achievement.

The first step to improve this process is to develop an assessment plan that begins with analyzing the data provided through mandatory state assessments. Generally, this is summative data that provides schools with basic information about the achievement status of their students across multiple years. Schools can use this information to examine student achievement trends that indicate how widespread the literacy issues are (e.g., 45% nonproficient versus 12% nonproficient) and identify areas in need of additional focus. Trend data can also be utilized to better understand the professional development needs of teachers for the coming year. For example, consistently low scores within the vocabulary portion of a state assessment may indicate a need for professional development and coaching to improve teachers' ability to provide high-quality vocabulary instruction.

Given the summative nature of most state assessments, schools also need to collect progress-monitoring data at consistent intervals to determine whether interventions are providing students with the support they need to meet literacy goals. We urge schools to rethink data collection from the traditional overreliance on high-stakes testing toward a more comprehensive system of data collection as a means of improving instruction. We also counsel schools to collect and examine data as a means of informing instruction rather than focusing solely on data as an evaluative tool (Carnegie Council on Advancing Adolescent Literacy, 2010). The purpose of data collection must go far beyond the assigning of a grade and instead should be regarded as an opportunity to gather critical information regarding student progress and the need for instructional changes. This information is critical not only for teachers but also for students, who must be regarded as at least equal partners in the learning process. Ultimately, maximizing student literacy outcomes will be possible only through consistent data collection and analysis and data-informed instructional decision making.

Teacher Support

Throughout this chapter, we have written about the importance of teachers delivering high-quality literacy instruction, designing literacy intervention programs, and using the data collection and analysis required to make data-informed instructional decisions. Given their critical importance, school leadership teams must work to ensure that teachers have the skills required to provide high-quality literacy instruction and intervention and to collect and analyze pertinent assessment data. Thus, it is essential that all comprehensive literacy action plans include a detailed plan for providing ongoing professional development and support for teachers to ensure that they possess the necessary skills required to maximize instructional effectiveness (Carnegie Council on Advancing Adolescent Literacy, 2010; Wise, 2009; Jacobs, 2008; Heller & Greenleaf, 2007). Unfortunately, a teacher support plan is often the most neglected aspect of a comprehensive literacy action plan. While it is not uncommon to find schools and districts offering isolated reading strategy professional development, it is rare to find schools and districts providing sustained professional development focused on cross-content literacy instruction based on analysis of student data. Well-designed literacy action plans must include ongoing professional development that meets the needs of all teachers, preparing them to meet the instructional needs of all students.

Another aspect often missing in literacy action plans is scheduled time for teachers to engage in collaborative discussion, lesson planning, and reflection (Wei, Darling-Hammond, Andree, Richardson, & Orphanos, 2009; Darling-Hammond, 2002). We cannot stress enough the importance of regularly scheduled time for teachers to plan collaboratively and reflect on their practice. Teachers need time to reflect and discuss with their peers the instructional changes they are expected to implement in their classrooms (Heller &

Greenleaf, 2007). As such, we, along with the Carnegie Council (2010) call on schools to "ensure that professional development is sustained, coherent, and comprehensive, meeting the needs of veteran and new teachers alike" and to provide time for "teacher teams to meet and discuss student data and progress" (p. 66).

Once time for teaming and reflection has been ensured, it is often best to include a skilled facilitator to support effective teaming and collaboration. Facilitators can guide teachers through the PS/RTI process to help them identify and define literacy problems, identify barriers to improving student learning, work together to augment instruction and intervention, and evaluate the impact of the instructional/intervention on student literacy outcomes. Supporting the problem-solving efforts of teachers results in more accurate identification of barriers, better buy-in to instructional/intervention plans, and improved instructional fidelity than when instructional/intervention plans are developed solely by the leadership team and imposed on teachers.

Finally, teacher support and professional development provided by highly trained instructional coaches yield the most effective, sustained instructional changes and are paramount to improving student achievement (Wei et al., 2009). Oftentimes, even when teachers have received high-quality professional development, they do not implement the suggested changes. This can occur for many reasons: teachers may be resistant to changes, may not understand reading development and, thus, the need for the changes, or may not have the skills to implement the changes without continuing support (Snow & Biancarosa, 2003). We recommend that well-trained instructional coaches provide ongoing support through an intensive coaching model that includes co-planning, modeling instruction, co-teaching, observing instruction, and debriefing. While we do not promote the intensive coaching cycle for all teachers, our experiences have supported implementing the intensive coaching model for teachers who are struggling with incorporating literacy instruction within their own lessons as an effective tool for sustaining instructional changes.

Conclusion

As you read through the remainder of this book, you will find specific examples of how to implement the initiatives suggested in this chapter. We recognize that the task is difficult and will require ongoing commitment. We believe, however, that the process of developing effective literacy action plans through a collaborative structure utilizing the PS/RTI framework will result in the cultural changes necessary to sustain student achievement.

2

The What and the Why of RTI

RTI—"Our Best Last Hope"
—Richard Allington, 2009

Type "response to intervention" into any search engine on the Internet, and literally millions of links to articles, commentaries, and resources appear. This fact stands in sharp contrast to memories of times, not too many years ago, when mention of response to intervention (RTI) at our schools was met with only blank stares and questions of "What is RTI?" and "What does that have to do with anything?" Today, most educators have at least heard the terms *problem solving* and *response to intervention,* and many have at least a cursory understanding of the RTI framework.

The surge of RTI knowledge is likely the result of the remarkable attention paid to RTI by the national education community as a means for reforming and improving schools, maximizing student outcomes, and reducing drop-out rates. A significant amount of discussion has occurred nationally and at state, district, and school levels regarding the implications of implementing an RTI framework as well as the associated concerns and costs. As a result, the term *RTI* has become rather common place among educators.

Unfortunately, despite ongoing professional dialogue, there remains great misunderstanding among educators, particularly at the secondary level, regarding the purpose, scope, and components of implementing an RTI framework. For instance, educators often associate RTI solely with excep-tional student education and see it as a means for identifying students eli-gible for special education services. At the secondary level, where exeptional student education eligibility is not a primary focus, many educators are still struggling to understand why RTI is worth the time and effort. When RTI is implemented at the secondary level, it is often in relation to remedial education and is rarely applied to address core instruction or seen as a vehicle to maximize school-wide outcomes. In contrast, we believe that RTI should be regarded as a vehicle for improving and maximizing the achievement of every student across all levels of the educational system. With this belief, we agree with Richard Allington's assessment that RTI is perhaps "our best last hope" (Rebora, 2010) for improving adolescent literacy and urge districts and schools to invest in ongoing professional development to increase the awareness and skills of secondary educators to implement a full RTI framework.

This chapter focuses on defining a working definition of RTI and outlines the key components of the RTI framework. Additionally, we discuss the implications of RTI at the secondary level for improving and maximizing school-wide literacy outcomes.

What Is RTI?

Response to intervention (RTI) is "the practice of providing high-quality instruction and interventions matched to student needs and using learning rate over time and level of performance to make important educational decisions" (Batsche et al., 2006). So what does this mean exactly? Let's dive deeper into each component of the definition.

Providing High-Quality Instruction/Intervention. High-quality instruction and intervention comprises two components: (1) research-based, best-practice instructional design and delivery and (2) evidence that, when implemented, the instruction/intervention is effective for the majority of local students (i.e., typically defined as 80% or more of students).

Research-based, best-practice instructional design and delivery is emphasized because these practices have the greatest likelihood of being effective. School teams should exercise caution when selecting research-based strategies and programs by ensuring that a true, independent research base exists and that the study participants are demographically similar to the school's student population. When these points are not fully considered up front, the results can be disastrous.

For instance, we can recall a school district that spent millions of dollars on a computer-based supplemental reading program that district leaders planned to implement across all their schools and with all their students. In order to understand the program better, we reviewed the available research. Unfortunately, what we found was virtually no independent research on the effectiveness of the program. Most of the research had been completed by the company that published the program, with the exception of a few articles that outlined some modest effects of improving the literacy outcomes of students with autism. When we met with the district leaders to discuss their implementation plan, they were shocked to find out that no independent research base existed that supported their plan to implement the program district-wide. Despite our shared concerns, the district moved forward with its implementation. We cautioned the district that implementing the program as planned was highly experimental and, thus, required close monitoring in order to measure and monitor the impact on student outcomes. The district agreed and implemented the program along with a plan to collect monthly progress-monitoring data from all the schools in order to evaluate the program's effectiveness. About midway through the year, it became apparent that the program was not achieving the desired results. Worse, at some schools, the program appeared to be having a negative impact on student outcomes. The program was discontinued at the end of the year. The district not only essentially threw away millions of dollars but also wasted a whole year implementing a program that was ineffective for its students.

There are two main takeaway lessons from this story. First and foremost, districts and schools must be prudent consumers and do their homework to determine what strategies and programs are truly research-based. Equally important, collecting evidence of the impact of instructional programming on student outcomes is the only way to be confident that the programming is effective for local students. Schools that wish to provide high-quality instruction/intervention must heed both lessons.

Matching Intervention to Student Needs. Far too often, we see schools design their instructional programs and allocate intervention resources without a clear understanding of what type of supports and resources the students need to be successful. Teachers provide lessons utilizing the same instructional strategies and curriculum materials year after year, even though their students, and consequently the needs of students, change every year. We often find that when students do not respond to core instruction, students, instead of the instruction, are viewed as the source of the problem, even when a significant percentage of students fail to master benchmarks (e.g., 20% or more).

Unfortunately, as with core instruction, teams often select intervention programs without fully understanding what types of support the students need to be successful. As a result, students who do respond adequately to core instruction are funneled into predetermined intervention programs regardless of whether the program is designed to address the individual student's needs. Students rarely receive more time than is available within the existing intervention programs as the amount of time devoted to intervention is seen as a constant. We have seen this scenario play out again and again within our most struggling schools, and the results are always less than desirable. Fortunately, teams can choose to operate in a different way. Consider the following example.

Imagine an educational environment in which the needs of students are identified early, understood by all, and referenced to inform the development of the school's master schedule and instructional/intervention programming. Within this school, time and instruction are seen as variables and are manipulated readily in order to ensure successful outcomes for all students. Students who require more time to master standards receive supplemental instruction during the school day. Teachers purposefully select curriculum materials to meet the needs of the students. Educators understand and meet students' nonacademic needs during the school day by providing advisement, mentoring, and instruction in social and academic skills (e.g., study skills, note taking, organization). This example represents what it truly means to match high-quality instruction to student needs.

Using Learning Rate and Level of Performance. Learning rate refers to growth over time. A student's rate of growth is most meaningful when it is compared to the expected or goal rate of growth. For instance, a school that wishes to improve the percentage of students who score proficient on the state's reading assessment from 45% to 65% within a one-year period needs to increase the percentage of proficient students by at least 10% by midyear to be on track for the end-of-year goal. Increasing the percentage of proficient students by less than 10% by midyear represents either a "poor" or an "insufficient" response to instruction. See Figure 2.1: Student Response Examples on page 18 for a graphical representation of "positive," "insufficient," and "poor" responses to instruction/intervention.

Measuring learning rate over time allows schools to estimate when they can expect to achieve the learning goal if they continue with the exact same instructional, curricular, and environmental conditions. Measuring learning rate over time for secondary-school students is especially important given the limited amount of time schools have to improve and maximize students' achievement outcomes. For instance, middle schools need to understand the rate of growth that must be achieved in order to meet their learning targets within three years for entering cohorts of students, for specific groups of students (e.g., Annual Yearly Progress (AYP) subgroups), and for individual students. Without examining the rate of learning over time in comparison to the rate required to meet the learning goal in the available time, teams sometimes celebrate "insufficient" responses. While they are pleased to see an upward

FIGURE 2.1 Student Response Examples

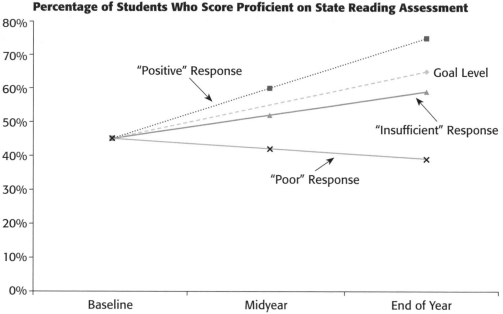

trend, they fail to recognize that they will not meet their learning goal within the specified time period without intensifying the instructional/intervention programming.

Equally important is a team's understanding of students' level of performance, which refers to the current performance level of students relative to the expected performance level. Level of performance plays an especially important role at the secondary level and should be used to inform initial placement of students into intervention programs. Unlike elementary settings, where it makes sense to first implement less-intense intervention with struggling students and utilize their individual response rates to determine whether a student is in need of more intense intervention, it makes more sense at the secondary level to provide students with the most intense needs with concentrated, targeted intervention immediately upon their entry (Fuchs, Fuchs, & Compton, 2010). Students enter middle and high schools with well-established skill deficits and gaps as well as high levels of disengagement that often accompany years of academic failure. Providing targeted intensive intervention for students who need it immediately upon their secondary-school entry likely will improve student outcomes by maximizing the amount of time students are exposed to the intervention (Fuchs et al., 2010) and reduce the likelihood that students will experience course failures and further disengagement.

Making Important Educational Decisions. Think about the number of important educational decisions required every year of educators from the state level to the school level, including the allocation of personnel, materials, time, and monetary resources from the state to the districts, from the districts to the schools, and from the schools to students. While many of these decisions are driven by complicated funding formulas at the state level, decisions regarding allocation of resources at the school level are often made via individual or team preference or opinion.

For instance, many schools divide their support personnel equally among classrooms or content areas in an attempt to be "fair" without fully considering whether specific classrooms and content areas (and the students within them) require more support than others. Other examples include the tendency for schools to create master schedules without first considering student needs, to place the least experienced and least qualified teachers within reading intervention classrooms, and to maximize the enrollment of intervention classrooms while allowing much smaller enrollment in advanced courses.

Conversely, within an RTI framework, all decisions are informed directly by student performance data (Batsche et al., 2006). Resources are allocated based on student need, which is determined by examining student performance levels and rates of growth. Students with lower performance levels and rates of growth are provided with the most intense resources (e.g., more time, smaller class size, most effective teachers, etc.).

What Is Required?

RTI is a framework that allows for effective strategic planning at every level of the educational system, from the state level to the individual student level. Unlike a program or curriculum that can be purchased with all the key components neatly marketed in shrink-wrap, RTI is a strategic-thinking and resource-allocation framework that requires consensus among educators and the building of critical infrastructure components (i.e., consensus, effective teaming, problem-solving skills, and multitiered systems of student supports).

Consensus. Change initiatives crucial to organizational success fail 70% of the time due to a lack of buy-in from those who are charged with implementation (Miller, 2002). Like with any school improvement or reform initiative, building consensus among educators regarding the implementation of an RTI framework is critical to its successful implementation. There are many facets of consensus building to which teams must attend, including the need for and focus of school improvement efforts, the expected improvements, and the impact of RTI on individual workloads and responsibilities. Educators must be provided with professional development to understand the RTI framework along with ongoing support for implementation. Additionally, allowing time up front and throughout the implementation process for educators to express their concerns and ask questions reduces anxiety levels and helps lead to consensus. Ultimately, when educators understand the need for and the benefits of RTI implementation and perceive that they have the skills and/or support to work successfully within the framework, consensus can be built and maintained.

Effective Teaming. Effective leadership teams and professional learning communities are essential for the successful implementation of an RTI framework and for school improvement in general. A thorough discussion regarding the development of a literacy leadership team is included in Chapter 3. This discussion centers around the ideas that effective teams (1) share clear goals for students, which helps focus their work, (2) collaborate regularly and perceive a collective responsibility for achieving goals, (3) problem solve barriers that preclude their students from achieving the learning targets, and (4) communicate with other school teams in order to influence their school's practices, decisions, and policies.

Informed Problem-Solving Skills and Processes. Regardless of the educational level, full RTI implementation requires the use of the problem-solving process (see Figure 2.2) to identify and analyze student achievement and engagement problems, to design and implement effective instructional/intervention plans, and to monitor the impact of instruction on student outcomes. The application of problem solving to school improvement efforts can help transform school teams, moving them quickly from a mode of reactivity to one of strategic planning and thoughtful reflection.

Problem Identification

The first step of the problem-solving process is problem identification. Within this step, academic and behavioral/engagement problems are defined as the difference between current and expected levels of performance. For example, a school may find that only 35% of students score proficient on the state reading assessment, while the expectation is that at least 80% of the students will score within the proficient range. The problem identification step of the problem-solving process is essential in that it allows teams to identify students in need of support and to determine the scope of the problem. It helps establish the

FIGURE 2.2 The Problem-Solving Process

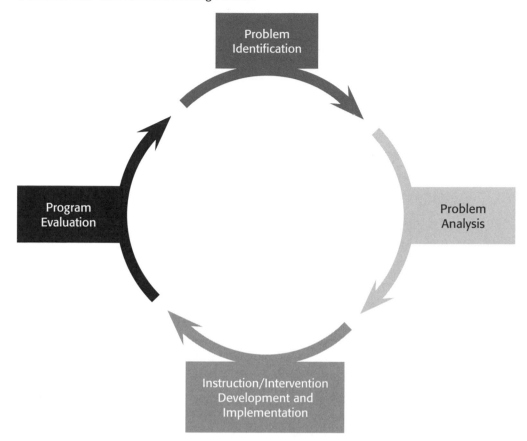

Reproduced with permission from Florida PS/RTI Project

reason for and focus of school improvement planning and determines the scope of intervention plans (e.g., Tier 1, Tier 2, and/or Tier 3 intervention).

Consider this example. It would make sense for a school in which 75% of students lack the necessary background knowledge and vocabulary development to master grade-level content to implement an intervention plan that supports all students by incorporating strategies for building background knowledge and content-specific vocabulary into core instruction. In contrast, a school with only 10% of students lacking sufficient background and vocabulary knowledge may choose to address this problem through small-group supplemental intervention. Identifying the scope of student literacy problems prior to planning for instruction allows teams to make informed decisions regarding the allocation of resources (e.g., master schedule development) to best meet the needs of the students and improve the likelihood of maximizing student literacy outcomes.

Without first understanding the breadth of the identified problem, teams have a tendency to spend their time problem solving around individual student issues, which is neither efficient nor particularly effective. Instead, school teams should devote their time to problem solving identified issues (e.g., literacy), particularly those that impact large numbers of students.

Determining the Gap

The difference between a student's or a group of students' current level of achievement or understanding and the expected level of achievement or understanding (i.e., learning goal) constitutes the achievement gap. To identify current achievement levels and determine achievement gaps, teachers must work to make student thinking visible so that students' level of understanding can be compared to the learning goal. Students' thinking can be made visible by reviewing written work, such as homework or in-class assignments; asking students to explain how they completed a task or solved a problem; observing a small collaborative group work; and/or administering a test that requires students to show or explain their work. Ideally, teachers should plan their data collection as part of the lesson-planning process. Determining the questions that will be asked at critical points during the lesson and the tasks that will be completed by students and reviewed by the teacher prior to teaching the lesson allows for the collection of student data to be more thoughtful and fluid than would be possible if such decisions were made on the spot during instruction.

Determining the gap between current and expected levels of student performance for groups of students (e.g., whole school, grade-level cohorts, AYP subgroups) is fairly straightforward. For instance, if 65% of students are proficient in reading and the expectation is that at least 80% of students are proficient in reading, then the gap between expected and current rates of proficiency is 15%.

Determining Why Gaps Exist. Determining why gaps exist is essential to planning and providing instruction that will close the gaps. For example, teachers may notice that students are not performing on unit exams or participating effectively in class discussions. Rather than continuing instruction, teachers should determine why students are struggling. One way to address this concern is to collect pre-test data to determine whether students possess knowledge of specific vocabulary words essential to the topic or concept being taught. Collecting pre-test data to identify students' understanding of essential vocabulary followed by providing explicit vocabulary instruction as part of the lesson and monitoring students' vocabulary acquisition throughout and at the end of the lesson cycle improves students' ability to understand the essential knowledge of the lesson.

Additionally, monitoring student learning throughout the lesson cycle may reveal that the students require an alternative instructional approach to learn the lesson vocabulary. A teacher may find that although he or she is explaining the vocabulary words in detail, many students are not acquiring the vocabulary nor are they able to explain the meaning of the vocabulary in their own words or correctly utilize the vocabulary words in a sentence. The teacher may conclude that the students require a visual prompt to understand the meaning of the vocabulary words. As a result, he or she may include pictures or videos within the explicit vocabulary instruction to make the meaning of the vocabulary words more clear for students. If only a few students fail to master the meaning of the vocabulary words, the teacher may then choose to target a small group of students and add visual supports and reteach the vocabulary as part of small-group instruction.

Teachers must not only collect data regarding student readiness for learning, student learning needs, and student progress but also use the data to make instructional decisions and adapt instruction to meet the needs of their students. Understanding the precise nature of student needs will be greatly enhanced by taking the time to fully analyze student data.

Problem Analysis

An understanding of student needs coupled with an understanding of the instructional, curricular, and environmental conditions that inhibit or accelerate student learning allows teachers to plan and adjust their instruction, the materials used during instruction, and the instructional environment to best meet the needs of their students. The process of analyzing the interaction between student needs and instructional, curricular, and environmental conditions is known as problem analysis and is the second step in the problem-solving process.

Problem analysis is an inductive process through which teams collect and analyze a range of relevant information across multiple domains (i.e., instruction, curriculum, environment, and learner) in order to better understand barriers or potential barriers to student success. The process allows school teams to better understand student intervention needs and to develop instructional programming designed to prevent academic and behavioral deficits from occurring in the first place (Fuchs et al., 2010). Analyzing identified problems to determine instructional, curricular, environmental, and learner variables that prevent students from achieving the expected levels of performance is essential to the development of effective intervention plans.

Unfortunately, problem analysis is perhaps the most often compromised or disregarded step of the problem-solving process (Hosp, 2008). Although problem analysis is often the most time-consuming step of the problem-solving process, spending time thoroughly analyzing the problem ultimately reduces the amount of time and effort wasted on the implementation of interventions that do not address the underlying reasons for the problem and have little or no chance of having the desired impact on student achievement.

Fully analyzing the identified problems sometimes requires teams to adjourn their meetings in order to collect additional information. While it's clear that data collection and analysis allows teams to better understand the root causes of problems before moving on to intervention planning and to maximize the likelihood of effective intervention planning, leaving the table before identifying "solutions" to the problem often leaves team members feeling very uncomfortable. This is especially true given the reactive nature of many secondary schools and the pressure placed on them by state and district accountability systems. Nonetheless, teams will find that the time spent engaging in problem-analysis activities is well worth the effort and temporary feelings of discomfort.

Teams that rush to find solutions for identified problems without thoroughly analyzing the problem often consider too few sources of information and tend to weight specific information (e.g., teacher interview data) more heavily than other relevant and important data. This common mistake can lead to an incomplete or even biased view of the barriers that caused or contributed to the identified problem. Another common mistake made by teams is the overemphasis on learner variables such as student motivation and parent involvement. Focusing primarily on learner variables, most of which are not directly alterable, is comforting for teams in the short term because the focus is temporarily directed toward students and parents and away from more personally held school-related variables. Unfortunately, this approach not only eventually leads to feelings of helplessness and frustration while reinforcing resentment toward students and parents but also virtually guarantees that effective instructional/intervention strategies will not be planned or implemented with fidelity.

Instead of focusing on student and family variables, teams need to consider all relevant variables that may cause or contribute to the problem. Collecting information utilizing the RIOT (Review, Interview, Observe, and Test) process (Figure 2.3) helps teams analyze problems more thoroughly and effectively (Hosp, 2006).

The acronym RIOT can help guide educators' decisions regarding the collection of relevant data and information. We often joke with school teams

FIGURE 2.3 RIOT

R	Review existing data and permanent products
I	Interview, survey, or question students, teachers, and other stakeholders
O	Observe the instructional environment, teachers, and students
T	Test, utilize formal and informal written formative assessments to gather student achievement/engagement data

that the letters *R*, *I*, *O*, and *T* are in that order not just because collecting data is so much fun (i.e., a riot) but also because they represent the least intrusive and resource-laden version of data collection (Review) to the most intrusive and most resource-laden version of data collection (Test). It goes without saying that if a team already has data that can be reviewed to answer a question, there is no need to collect additional information. In fact, this would constitute a waste of resources (time, energy, etc.).

Although this seems obvious, we continue to see schools collecting data (typically through testing) to answer questions to which they already have the answers. For example, we recently worked with a school that spent one full day a month testing its students' reading skills, resulting in a significant amount of lost instructional time. When we inquired about the data that was being collected every month, we were handed a list of 14 assessments that were administered to every student in the building. Upon further analysis, we found that 10 of the assessments were measures of reading comprehension, and the remaining four were measures of vocabulary knowledge, encoding (to assess phonics), and fluency. When we pointed this fact out to the school leaders, they insisted that they had no choice but to administer all assessments because it was a district mandate. They lamented that the time spent assessing students not only interfered with instruction but also left very little time to analyze the data or use the information to inform instruction. As a result, the school was collecting massive amounts of student assessment data that were never analyzed sufficiently and were rarely used to improve instruction.

We were, of course, very concerned with this situation and arranged to meet with the school and district leadership teams with the hope of developing a more efficient data collection plan. Working collaboratively, the teams agreed to collect new information only when a question could not be answered by reviewing already existing information. For instance, the team discovered that roughly 60% of the student population scored proficient or above on the state's reading assessment at the end of the previous year, demonstrating that the students possessed sufficient reading skills to comprehend grade-level text. Thus, it was unnecessary to collect new information every month to determine whether or not these students had intact reading comprehension skills. Further, one could assume that these students also possessed sufficient vocabulary knowledge, decoding skills, and reading fluency to allow for the comprehension of grade-level text. Thus, assessing the students in these areas was unnecessary. As a result, the team decided to stop administering targeted diagnostic assessments with students who had demonstrated proficiency on the general outcome measure (i.e., reading comprehension).

Further, the team decided to collect new information about the 60% of students demonstrating proficiency only three times per year in order to answer the question, "Are the students progressing at a rate sufficient to master reading standards at their current grade level by the end of the year?" The team also agreed that the 40% of students who did not demonstrate proficiency on the previous year's state reading assessment, all of whom were receiving reading intervention, would receive diagnostic assessments in order to better understand their underlying reading issues (e.g., decoding, vocabulary, fluency) that made grade-level text comprehension difficult or impossible. This information would be used to plan more targeted, and likely more effective, reading intervention programs. Instead of ten reading comprehension assessments each month, the most proficient students (i.e., the 60% of students who scored proficient the previous year) would be administered one assessment three times a year. Nonproficient students would be administered diagnostic assessments to better understand their reading issues and monthly progress-monitoring assessments to track their progress.

The school's new assessment plan saved a considerable amount of time and energy, as well as other resources, such as copy costs, while allowing the school to monitor the growth and progress of all students over time. A portion of this saved time was devoted to analyzing the data and utilizing the information gleaned to plan instruction and intervention. Also, because the school was no longer assessing all students monthly, there were resources available to conduct more thorough and comprehensive diagnostic assessments with students who were significantly behind in reading.

Instructional/Intervention Design and Implementation

Once a school team has gained an understanding of how widespread the literacy issues are (e.g., percentage of students scoring less than proficient) as well as barriers that have prevented students from meeting literacy goals, instructional/intervention planning is usually quite straightforward. As an example, if a team finds that 50% of its students have not mastered grade-level literacy standards because many students lack the content vocabulary necessary to comprehend grade-level text, it makes sense to intensify core vocabulary instruction for all students. Trying to develop intervention plans for each student individually is both inefficient and most likely ineffective given the near impossibility of supporting and monitoring hundreds of individualized intervention plans. A plan that includes infusing explicit vocabulary instruction across all content courses and within reading intervention time as well, for students who require more than core instruction to master grade-level vocabulary expectations, would be the most efficient approach and allow the team to adequately support and monitor implementation fidelity.

It is equally important for teams to be knowledgeable about research-based instructional/intervention strategies and programs when developing the school's literacy programming. To the extent possible, teams should implement scientifically validated instruction/interventions in order to ensure that students have access to instruction that has proven to be effective with other (preferably similar) students. Research-based interventions not only provide the best opportunity for students to receive the support they need but also are required by both the Individuals with Disabilities Education Act (IDEA) 2004 and the Elementary and Secondary Education Act (ESEA) 2010.

Unfortunately, selecting research-based instructional/intervention strategies is more difficult at the secondary level because there are far fewer proven strategies/programs for adolescent readers. A review of scientifically validated reading programs on the What Works Clearinghouse (WWC) Web site reveals 40 scientifically validated reading programs for elementary school students, six programs for middle school students, and only five for high school students. Further, while there are eight elementary-focused reading programs that have earned WWC's highest rating of "positive effects," none of the middle or high school reading programs have earned this designation and are instead categorized as "potentially positive." The limited number of scientifically proven reading programs for adolsecent students presents a challenge for literacy teams. Despite this challenge, teams should strive to choose instructional/intervention programming that has proven to have positive effects for adolescent learners. If a decision is made to implement instructional/intervention programming that has a limited research base, the team should regard the implementation as experimental and increase the frequency of progress monitoring in order to establish its own evidence base.

Multitiered System of Student Supports. Multitiered support systems typically comprise three tiers of increasingly intense supports that include Tier 1 core instruction, Tier 2 supplemental intervention, and Tier 3 targeted intervention. All students should receive core literacy instruction (Tier 1) regardless of their reading level. Even advanced students likely need literacy instruction to comprehend the highly complicated text utilized in their advanced courses, including vocabulary instruction and application of comprehension strategies. Without question, less advanced students require core literacy instruction to master grade-level literacy and content area standards. This instruction should occur within every content area classroom and include vocabulary and reading comprehension instruction and content area writing instruction. A complete discussion of core literacy instruction is provided in Chapter 5.

Tier 2 supplemental instruction is provided in addition to core instruction in order to address gaps in reading skill and to provide additional time and practice for students who need it to master grade-level standards. As with Tier 1 initial instruction, the goal of Tier 2 instruction is mastery of grade-level standards. Thus, Tier 2 instruction must be designed with a thorough understanding of Tier 1 goals as well as an analysis of the barriers that stand in the way for student mastery of those goals. Tier 2 instruction is more intense than Tier 1 instruction because it typically provides more explicit skill instruction within a smaller group size (e.g., five to ten students). A school is not likely to be able to support more than approximately 15% to 20% of its students within supplemental instruction. Attempts to serve more than 20% of the student population in a supplemental fashion likely will result in diluted intervention programs and overly taxed intervention providers. Schools that find more than 20% of their students are demonstrating literacy issues should address these concerns by intensifying core instruction.

Tier 3 targeted intervention is even more intense than Tier 2 instruction and is designed to meet the individual needs of students through a personalization of intervention supports. This level of personalization requires an intimate understanding of each individual student's academic and engagement needs. As with Tier 2 intervention, Tier 3 intervention is provided in addition to Tier 1 core instruction and should be designed to support each student's mastery of grade-level standards. Tier 3 intervention is typically provided within a very small group setting (e.g., two to four students) or individually and provides students with very explicit instruction. As with Tier 2 instruction, the purpose of Tier 3 intervention is to close any existing skill gaps a student may have while supporting the mastery of literacy standards within content area classes. Given the intensity, Tier 3 intervention requires substantial resource allocation (e.g., time, personnel). A school is unlikely to be able to support more than 5% of its students within Tier 3 interventions. Attempts to serve more than approximately 5% of students within Tier 3 interventions likely will result in a loss of the personalization and intervention intensity required to close significant literacy skill gaps and prevent content course failures that often result from the unaddressed literacy needs of students.

Instruction Before Intervention

Most school, district, and state initiatives rest on the premise that struggling readers need intensive interventions provided in reading intervention courses. The result has been to reinforce the misperception that reading is something taught outside of and separate from content courses. This commonly held misconception has led schools to attempt to intervene with struggling students without addressing shortcomings of core instruction as a whole.

It has become increasingly clear to us in our work with schools that building literacy intervention programs without maximizing the effectiveness of core literacy instruction results in overtaxed intervention providers and severely diluted intervention programs, which have little hope of providing the intensity of instruction required to remediate the majority of struggling readers. The result is that few students exit intervention classes while more students are added to the classes with each successive year. Consequently, secondary schools often are forced to devote increasing amounts of school resources to intervention over time.

We have seen this scenario play out again and again in the schools we support. All the high schools in which we work found they needed to incorporate into their master schedules more time for reading intervention for tenth grade than for ninth grade. In fact, by tenth grade, most of the schools reported that more than 50% of their students were placed in reading intervention classrooms. The drain on school resources was substantial and way too high a price to pay for largely ineffective literacy intervention. Our experience firmly confirms our belief that schools cannot intervene their way out of the responsibility of providing effective core literacy instruction.

Instead of an intervention-focused literacy program, effective literacy programming begins with the intensification of core literacy instruction. This is not to say that schools should not anticipate the need to provide more intense Tier 2 and Tier 3 intervention. In fact, most secondary schools need to plan for and implement supplemental (Tier 2) and targeted (Tier 3) intervention services for at least a portion of their student population. Tier 3 intervention, which typically provides a narrower instructional focus and smaller student grouping than Tier 2 intervention, should be reserved for students who demonstrate substantial reading deficits or whose progress-monitoring data indicates that they are not responsive to less-intense intervention.

Program Evaluation

Collecting ongoing progress-monitoring data in order to assess the effectiveness of literacy instruction and intervention is essential. Evaluating the impact of literacy programming on student outcomes allows teams to identify ineffective instruction and intervention, make timely instructional changes, and identify students who require more intensive intervention support. Comparing students' rate of progress to the rate required to close the "current level–expected level" gap is the first step in determining the adequacy of literacy programming.

Student response to instruction/intervention is considered "positive" if the rate of student growth matches or exceeds the rate required to eliminate the gap. This type of response signifies that the literacy programming will be sufficient in achieving the goal within the target period if the instruction/interventions continue to be implemented with fidelity. "Poor" responses are represented by flat or negative growth rates and indicate that the literacy programming is ineffective or even harmful to student literacy outcomes. Literacy programming that results in "poor" student responses should be augmented to better meet the needs of students.

At times, student outcome data indicates that learning is "insufficient" to allow for students to meet the identified goal within the goal period. This type of response may signify that the school team has selected the correct literacy programming to meet the needs of students, but instruction/intervention must be delivered at a greater intensity to meet the goal within the target time period. Intensification of literacy programming may include devoting more time to instruction, assigning additional personnel to allow for smaller student groups and differentiation, incorporating literacy instruction across a greater proportion of content courses, or incorporating positive reinforcement for students who demonstrate growth and/or achieve agreed-upon literacy goals.

Data-Informed Problem Solving

Collecting and analyzing student data is essential to every step of the problem-solving process, from the identification of skill gaps to the evaluation of literacy programming. Teams that spend time analyzing student data in order to develop an understanding of the literacy needs of their students and the instructional, curricular, and environmental conditions that maximize student progress are more likely to develop effective literacy programs.

In order to engage in data-informed problem solving, teams need to collect, manage, and analyze relevant student data. In addition to collecting and compiling the student data, teams should spend their time interpreting the data and applying what is learned to instructional/intervention planning. Adopting a set of guiding questions to direct the interpretation and application of student data, such as those outlined in Figure 2.4, can help standardize the interpretation of data, inform the decision-making process, and keep teams focused on the problem-solving process.

FIGURE 2.4 Guiding Questions for Tier 1, Tier 2, and Tier 3 Problem Solving

Guiding Questions for Solving Tier 1 Problems
1. Is the core program sufficient to meet the school-wide goals?
2. For which students is the core program sufficient or not sufficient?
3. What is preventing the core program from being sufficient; what are the barriers?
4. How will student needs and identified barriers be addressed within the core program?
5. How will the effectiveness and efficiency of the core program be monitored over time?
6. Have improvements to the core program been effective?
7. Which students need more intensive instruction to be successful?
8. What specific supplemental and intensive instruction is needed?
Guiding Questions for Solving Tier 2 and Tier 3 Problems
1. For which students is the core program not sufficient?
2. What barriers exist that have prevented the students from meeting expectations with core instruction alone?
3. What specific supplemental and intensive instruction is needed to meet the needs of students and remove the identified barriers?
4. How will specific supplemental and intensive instruction be delivered?
5. How will the effectiveness of supplemental and intensive instruction be monitored?
6. How effective is our supplemental and intensive instruction?
7. Which students need more intensive intervention to be successful?

Adapted from Heartland, Iowa's Data-Based Decision Making Questions (Heartland Area Education Agency, 2007)

Assessment Plans

In order to guarantee that teams have all the necessary data to make data-informed decisions, schools should develop assessment plans that outline what data will be collected, when, and for what purpose. Data are used to inform all steps of the problem-solving process, including the use of universal screening to identify and define student achievement problems, diagnostic data to better understand barriers to academic success, and progress-monitoring data to monitor the impact of instruction and intervention. Thus, assessment plans should include a school's plan to collect and analyze universal screening, diagnostic, and progress-monitoring data. Figure 2.5 (page 34) offers an assessment plan example that is utilized by one of the schools in which we work.

Universal Screening. Although the identification of students in need of intervention support is essential at both the elementary and the secondary school levels, there are significant differences regarding the specific data used to make such determinations. Unlike in elementary schools, where RTI models rely heavily on universal screening measures to identify students who are at risk for reading failure, secondary school teams typically have the benefit of multiple years of student data, making the administration of additional universal screening measures unnessesary. A review of existing data most often paints a very clear picture of the intensity and severity of reading problems for individual students, specific groups of students, and the student body as a whole. Thus, the best universal screening tool is a systematic data review protocol.

Diagnostic Assessments. Once students who are reading below grade level have been identified through a review of existing data, school teams should turn their atttention to better understanding why the students are experiencing difficulty. As with younger children, adolescents have difficulty reading for a variety of reasons. For instance, two students may receive the same score on the state assessment or another measure of reading comprehension but for two different underlying reasons. While state assessments and other measures of reading comprehension help teams determine the intensity of reading problems (i.e., the difference between students' current level and grade level), they do not typically provide information regarding why students are reading below grade level. The underlying reasons for reading problems are best uncovered through the administration of diagnostic assessments.

Teams can use diagnostic assessments to help distinguish among students who have difficulty reading due to decoding or word attack problems from those whose word attack skills are intact but who have issues reading fluently enough to allow for comprehension. Teachers can also use diagnostic assessments to help identify issues related to a lack of vocabulary, background knowledge, comprehension strategies, and engagement levels. Diagnostic assessments are essential to the planning and implementation of effective reading interventions. Rather than grouping by reading level, teachers should group students for intervention based on the common underlying reason for their reading problems and provide intervention specific to students' identified needs.

Progress Monitoring. In addition to the end-of-year state assessment, schools should administer a standards-based formative assessment at least three times a year to all students, to assess their overall competence in reading. The information gathered through these assessments allows teams to determine the needs of and progress made by the student body as a whole, specific groups of students (e.g., students with disabilities), and individual students. Schools should use this information to determine whether the instructional program should be continued as is, refined, expanded, or discontinued altogether.

More frequent progress monitoring is required for nonproficient students than for proficient students, particularly those whose reading skills are substantially deficient. In addition to monitoring reading comprehension, teachers should closely track student skill development relative to students' specific subskill deficit (e.g., decoding, fluency). At a minimum, teams should monitor the progress of students in need of Tier 2 and/or Tier 3 intervention support biweekly and compare the results to short-term learning goals to determine the sufficiency of programming. With this information, teams can make modifications to the reading intervention program for students who are not making sufficient progress toward their goals.

Why RTI?

In an ideal world, all students would enter secondary schools having mastered the reading process and with the ability to comprehend highly complex text. If this were the case, there would be no holes in their knowledge or skills, and they would be sufficiently prepared to read to learn within their content classes.

Unfortunately, this is not the reality. In fact, according to the National Assessment of Educational Progress (NAEP), approximately 25% of U.S. 12th graders read below the "basic" level, and that percentage does not even account for students who have already dropped out of school. More than half of students enter secondary schools without the knowledge and literacy skills fundamental to grade-level work. As a result, students without sufficient

FIGURE 2.5 Assessment Plan Example

Assessment Type	Whom to Assess	Assessment Tool	Assessment Purpose	Assessment Frequency
Universal screening	All students grades 6–12	Review of existing data	Identify students whose historical reading data indicate risk for reading failure.	Before developing master schedule and upon intake of a new student
Broad diagnostic assessments	All students grades 6–12	Measures of academic progress: Reading	Assess students' abilities to recognize words, decipher word meanings, comprehend text (literal and inferential/interpretive), and analyze and respond to text.	Three times per year (beginning, middle, and end of year)
Supplemental diagnostic assessment	Students whose broad screen assessments indicate below-level reading skills	MAZE	Assess students' accuracy, fluency, and basic comprehension skills.	Monthly
		Word analysis	Assess students' knowledge of the phonological, orthographical, and morphological information required to accurately identify words in text.	

FIGURE 2.5 Assessment Plan Example *(continued)*

Assessment Type	Whom to Assess	Assessment Tool	Assessment Purpose	Assessment Frequency
Targeted diagnostic assessment	Students who are reading significantly below grade level (e.g., two or more years)	Phonics surveys	Assess students' knowledge of letter-sound correspondences, orthographical characteristics, syllable patterns, prefixes, suffixes, and root words.	Weekly to biweekly; aligned with focus of intervention
		Oral reading fluency probes	Assess students' reading efficiency, including phrasing, intonation, expression, smoothness, and pace.	
		Scaffolded discussion templates*	Assess student comprehension skills while controlling for decoding skill deficits.	
Targeted diagnostic assessment		Academic word inventory	Assess student's context-free word reading ability.	Weekly to biweekly; aligned with focus of intervention
		Sight word inventory	Assess known sight words and ability to identify new words.	
		Literacy process interview	Assess the strategies students use for reading or writing.	

*From Florida Assessment for Instruction in Reading

FIGURE 2.5 Assessment Plan Example *(continued)*

Assessment Type	Whom to Assess	Assessment Tool	Assessment Purpose	Assessment Frequency
Progress monitoring	Students receiving reading intervention	Skill-specific (e.g., reading fluency, phonics, reading comprehension strategy application)	Monitor student response to skill-specific reading interventions.	Weekly
	All students	General outcome (i.e., reading comprehension)	Monitor student response to literacy instruction, including the impact of skill-specific intervention on reading comprehension.	At least three times per year for all students

Monthly for students receiving reading intervention |
| Ongoing informal formative assessment | All students | Higher-order questions, classroom-based assessments, observation of student discussions, etc. | Monitor student response to instruction for the purpose of ongoing, timely changes to instruction, including differentiation and appropriate scaffolding. | Ongoing, daily |

literacy skills are more likely to fail content courses and drop out of high school (Hammond, Linton, Smink, & Drew, 2007).

The RTI framework is aimed at preventing students from experiencing academic or engagement problems through the implementation of effective, research-based core instruction for all students and the provision of efficient and effective intervention for students who require more than core instruction to master academic and behavioral expectations. RTI rests firmly on the belief that given sufficient academic and behavioral instruction and support, all students can learn to meet academic and behavioral expectations. As educators, it is our responsibility to identify and provide the instructional, curricular, and environmental conditions that best enable the learning of all students. Secondary schools can no longer behave as if the responsibility for teaching students to read falls solely on elementary educators. Instead, districts and schools must adopt a framework that maximizes their capacity to provide effective instruction and intervention for all students.

Secondary schools must examine their reading trend data and communicate more comprehensively with their feeder schools, which will allow them to anticipate the literacy needs of their incoming students and to build responsive literacy programs. The ability of middle and high schools to deliver effective instructional/intervention literacy programs is greatly enhanced by understanding the precise needs of students, particularly those of the incoming sixth-grade and freshman classes. With this information, secondary schools can design and implement literacy programs that are customized to the needs of their particular student body before the effects of literacy problems (e.g., failed content courses) increase the likelihood of students dropping out (Kennelly & Monrad, 2007).

Implementing an RTI framework has important implications for secondary schools and helps them identify students in need of intervention earlier and provide more appropriate and effective instruction and intervention. Recognizing the potential positive impact of implementing an RTI framework on maximizing student literacy outcomes, the International Reading Association (IRA) recently formed a commission on RTI to provide educators with additional information and guidance regarding the use of an RTI framework to prevent and intervene with literacy and language related learning issues. The IRA Commission on Response to Intervention described RTI as "a comprehensive, systemic approach to teaching and learning designed to address language and literacy problems for all students through increasingly differentiated and intensified language and literacy assessment and instruction" (p. 1) and proposed six key principles to guide the implementation of RTI as it relates to language and literacy instruction and intervention (see Figure 2.6: IRA's Six Key RTI Principles on page 38).

FIGURE 2.6 IRA's Six Key RTI Principles

IRA's Six Key RTI Principles

Principle 1: Instruction
RTI is first and foremost intended to prevent language and literacy problems by optimizing instruction.

Principle 2: Responsive Teaching and Differentiation
The RTI process emphasizes increasingly differentiated and intensified instruction/intervention in language and literacy.

Principle 3: Assessment
An RTI approach demands assessment that can inform language and literacy instruction meaningfully.

Principle 4: Collaboration
RTI requires a dynamic, positive, and productive collaboration among professionals with relevant expertise in language and literacy. Success also depends on strong and respectful partnerships among professionals, parents, and students.

Principle 5: Systemic and Comprehensive Support
RTI must be part of a comprehensive, systemic approach to language and literacy assessment and instruction and should provide support for all K–12 students.

Principle 6: Expertise
All students have the right to receive instruction from well-prepared teachers who keep up-to-date and supplemental instruction from professionals specifically prepared to teach language and literacy, as noted in IRA's statement "Making a Difference Means Making It Different: Honoring Children's Rights to Excellent Reading Instruction."

International Reading Association, 2010

The key principles provided by IRA align perfectly with our conceptualization of how an RTI framework can be used to maximize student literacy outcomes, including the importance of vertical programming to prevent literacy problems, the use of assessment data to inform and improve core literacy instruction, and the importance of collaboration among professionals to improve literacy instruction/intervention from kindergarten through graduation.

Conclusion

Effective literacy programming requires a whole-school approach within which all school personnel understand their roles and responsibilities. A multitiered system of student supports maximizes the likelihood that all students will receive the intensity of intervention matched to their needs. School teams must understand the common literacy needs of their student body and plan Tier 1 core instruction accordingly. The implementation of an RTI framework helps prevent school teams from making the common mistake of attempting to intervene with struggling readers without addressing shortcomings of core instruction as a whole.

Building strong Tier 1 core literacy programs and accompanying intervention supports for students who need them is essential to meeting the needs of all students. This shift requires strong instructional leadership, collective ownership of school-wide literacy goals, and a commitment to cross-content literacy instruction. Improving the effectiveness of core literacy instruction can substantially reduce the number of students who are at risk for or experience reading difficulties. Thus, in order to improve student achievement, all teachers must first understand the specific needs of their students and accordingly address the literacy needs of students through effective instruction, which includes direct, explicit, cross-content literacy instruction.

3

Transforming Your Literacy Leadership Team into a Problem-Solving Team

The most promising strategy for substantive school improvement is developing the capacity of school personnel to function as a professional learning community.

—Eaker, DuFour, & DuFour, 2002

Developing a highly functioning literacy leadership team (LLT) is the first step toward getting serious about adolescent literacy. This is especially true for secondary schools because it is virtually impossible to change student achievement without first addressing school culture and accelerating the rate of adult learning as it relates to student literacy. Effective LLTs are instrumental in promoting awareness of the impact of literacy on student learning and academic outcomes and in providing support to enable teachers to make the instructional, curricular, and environmental changes necessary to meet the literacy needs of all students. Highly functional literacy leadership teams serve as a driving force behind substantive instructional change initiatives and work to develop staff commitment to and capacity for the sustained continuous improvement required to maximize student literacy outcomes over time.

Establishing an effective LLT does not just happen. School leadership must take time to establish the team and allow the team sufficient time for careful analysis of student, teacher, and school-wide data; identification of school-based instructional, curricular, and environmental barriers that impact literacy outcomes; design and implementation of research-based instruction and intervention plans to lessen or remove the impact of identified barriers;

and establishment and implementation of an evaluation plan to determine student response to instruction/intervention that allows for modification of plans as needed. This chapter will focus on establishing the LLT and supporting the team's data-informed problem solving efforts.

Establishing the Team

Establishing a functional LLT is critical to the success of any literacy initiative or action plan. The scope of the LLT's work (i.e., problem solve literacy issues and develop literacy plans to be implemented across content areas) requires the LLT to function differently from most school committees whose work is typically more narrowly focused and applied. To accomplish its mission, the LLT must work collaboratively to pinpoint literacy issues, identify barriers to meeting literacy goals, engage in research and discussion regarding possible solutions for addressing identified concerns and barriers, and monitor the impact of the literacy plan on student outcomes. As such, serving on the LLT requires a significant time commitment and a willingness to put into practice and support instructional/intervention plans identified as having the greatest likelihood of resulting in improved student achievement. This mission of the LLT is immense and of utmost importance. Consequently, we recommend that schools proceed with great care and intentionality when forming and managing their LLTs to ensure success.

Identifying Team Members. Ensuring successful LLT outcomes requires principals to carefully consider potential candidates. Ideally, the team includes stakeholders from across the school, including administrators, content area and/or grade-level team members, instructional coaches, and support staff. The goal is to establish a representative team of committed individuals who are interested in and passionate about promoting literacy across the curriculum.

Effective members are those who are recognized as instructional leaders within the school community as well as those who have demonstrated success improving student achievement. School leaders should identify potential members who have a track record of effective communication with members of the faculty, who are known for their willingness to share ideas, and who are willing to consider the ideas of others. It's important to remember that the most vocal teachers may not always be the most effective teachers or teacher leaders. Instead of including only the most vocal teachers, school leaders should include teachers who not only have a good rapport with their students but also are able to work well with and are respected by other teachers.

An LLT should include teachers from across the curriculum to ensure that each content area is represented in the literacy planning process. Structuring the team in this way improves buy-in to the literacy plan from teachers across the various content areas and improves fidelity of implementation. While our goal is to develop capacity within the school to promote literacy instruction and improve student achievement, it is not necessary or wise to limit team members to those who are experts in adolescent literacy. Instead, members may include those who have shown an interest in understanding how to improve student achievement and are willing to engage in their own professional development as a means for improving their own instruction. The team should not be limited to those who believe they already have the answers. Instead, school leaders should fill the team with those who are searching for the answers.

Principals should take time to individually invite members to join the team and share with them that they have been personally selected in recognition of their past performance and commitment to improving student outcomes. School leaders should remind potential candidates that the LLT is not a "committee" that meets monthly to review information. Instead, LLT members must be committed not only to attending the meetings but also to engaging in professional development, action research, and problem solving as a means of improving literacy instruction across the curriculum. When principals take the time to personally invite members and explain the importance their role will have on improving the school culture, members begin to understand the significance of the commitment they are being asked to consider and demonstrate more consistent commitment to the team's mission over time.

Finally, we believe that the most important member of the LLT is the school principal. If the goals are to truly impact school-wide culture and effectively improve instruction, the principal must fully participate as a member of the LLT. The time spent engaging in collegial conversation with members of the team is invaluable. The school principal's involvement ensures that he or she understands the problem-solving process and the resulting instructional/intervention plan, has an opportunity to allocate critical resources to support the plan, and recognizes how to support implementation fidelity via coaching and monitoring. As a school principal once shared, it is difficult for principals to monitor implementation of initiatives unless they completely understand the reasoning behind and purpose of the initiatives. It is also difficult or even impossible to allocate sufficient resources without the benefit of understanding precisely what resources will be needed to initiate and sustain the literacy plan. With this understanding, we strongly recommend that the LLT membership include the school's principal.

Developing a Collegial Community. Once the team has been assembled, it should arrange for quality time to establish team norms and develop a sense of community and shared commitment within the team. It's not unusual for teams to want to skip the process of determining team norms and communication plans or establishing consensus around the team's mission and goals. This is particularly common among group members who perceive they have worked well together in other contexts and may see the time spent on such activities as wasteful. However, the value of team norms is often most evident during times of disagreement or conflict. While it is true that team members may naturally respect one another's input and influence on the group when there is relative agreement, balancing the ideas of each team member when disagreements arise is much more difficult without agreed-upon group norms to reference. In this scenario, group norms serve as a protective factor for the overall team's cohesion and functioning.

In addition to establishing group norms, LLTs should develop a clearly articulated communication plan. The plan should include how the team members will communicate with one another (i.e., mode, frequency, topics) as well as how the team will communicate with the school's leadership team and content area teams (i.e., mode, frequency, topics). The communication plan will help ensure that the school's leadership team and content area teams are aware of the LLT's work, mission, goals, and needs. Establishing what and when information will be shared outside the group will allow team members to be transparent about their concerns and ideas and to have control over the information to be shared with other important school teams. The most successful schools commit to a minimum of a full-day off campus in order to build relationships within the team, create a vision for the team, identify areas of concern, and begin the process of professional development in order to determine the best interventions. Developing team norms is essential to ensuring effective team meetings.

Norms to consider include the following:

- ◆ Establish time commitments.
- ◆ Agree to fully listen while others are sharing.
- ◆ Interact with team members respectfully.
- ◆ Fully participate in the conversation.
- ◆ Attend all meetings and team activities.
- ◆ Engage in personal professional development and action research to determine the effectiveness of identified team initiatives.

This first session is followed by two or three additional days to develop a comprehensive action plan. Depending on the time of year, these first meetings should take place either off campus if school is in session or over the summer during preplanning (Craig, 2010).

If possible, a skilled facilitator should guide the conversation and help develop team protocols. If including an outside facilitator is not possible, a team member who has successfully served as a facilitator on other school teams and who is comfortable serving as a guide and not as a director can act as facilitator. The team might consider including team-building activities that allow members to get acquainted, engage in conversations, and share goals and expectations for the team. The goal is to develop an expectation of professional engagement in collegial discussion and research and to develop an action plan that best serves the needs of the school's students.

Identifying the Team's Mission and Goals. Once the team is established, it is time to engage in discussion to determine the school LLT's mission and related goals. The LLT mission and goals should relate directly to the mission of the school in general and the school-wide vision for improving literacy across the curriculum. This can best be accomplished by providing activities that allow members to engage in small-group conversation followed by whole-group discussion. Allowing time for the members to work collaboratively in small groups ensures that all members have a voice and feel comfortable sharing concerns and ideas.

Eaker, Dufour, & Dufour (2002) suggest the first conversation should focus on the school's vision. Ask the team to discuss the following questions:

◆ Why do we exist as a school?
◆ What kind of school do we hope to become?
◆ How must we behave in order to create the kind of school we hope to become?

Take time to carefully articulate a team response to each of these questions. The most powerful of the three is the last question, "How must we behave in order to create the kind of school we hope to become?" Discussion focused on this question helps set the tone for the purpose and mission of the LLT. In order for the team to meet its collective goals, each member must be willing to abide by a set of agreed-upon best practices, make any necessary changes within their classrooms, and assist teachers with the change process and with the implementation of the literacy plan.

In addition to a common mission, vision, and collective commitments, the LLT must also establish literacy goals. Taking time to determine specific, measurable goals before jumping into brainstorming solutions leads to more focused and targeted problem solving. Teams that work to collaboratively and collegially identify and establish the mission, vision, and goals for the school-wide literacy initiatives are more likely to develop, implement, and maintain successful action plans than teams that skip these important team development steps. These components are essential and serve as the foundation for the team's ability to effectively problem solve barriers to achieving literacy goals.

After establishing the LLT's mission, vision, and goals, the team should engage in a careful discussion of literacy (Craig, 2010), especially as it relates to each teacher's individual content area. Asking members to consider what it means to be a literate scientist versus a literate mathematician or how reading literature differs from reading historical text are important concepts to examine early on in developing team goals and foster buy-in to the action planning process. Questions to consider include these:

- ◆ What does it mean to be literate in my content area?
- ◆ What skills must students demonstrate to become literate in my content area?
- ◆ How might my instruction need to change in order to prepare students to be literate in my content area?

Note again that the most important question is the last question, "How might my instruction need to change in order to prepare students to be literate in my content area?" As members begin to discuss the necessary changes within individual content areas, they also will begin to examine commonalities that exist between content areas (e.g., vocabulary development) that can be used to develop school-wide goals.

Problem Solving/Response to Intervention

Addressing student literacy achievement is a complicated task that requires careful consideration of the myriad of factors impacting adolescent literacy. We will discuss in depth student motivation, literacy instruction, development of a multitiered system of support, and teacher support throughout the chapters that follow. Our intent here is to provide structures for analyzing data to inform the problem-solving process.

Clearly, the first step toward determining a need and focus for school-wide literacy instruction and intervention is to examine student reading achievement data. Central to the data analysis process is the development of a clear understanding of the difference between expected and current levels of student reading achievement. Team members who do not understand this gap will likely not see a need to implement different or additional instructional or intervention literacy supports for students. Consensus around the need to make changes to the school's current literacy program will be achieved only when all team members have had the opportunity to review students' current levels of reading achievement, discuss expected levels of achievement, and determine the gap between the two.

Perhaps not surprisingly, the process of thoroughly analyzing existing student reading data and determining the gap between the current and expected achievement levels can be emotionally taxing on teams and team members. This may be particularly true for those who are heavily invested in or are seen by others as responsible for student reading outcomes (e.g., reading coaches, reading teachers, literacy specialists). It is not uncommon for team members to feel angry, defensive, or depressed regarding their ability to impact student literacy outcomes. Referring back to the team norms that focus on mutual respect and collective ownership of student outcomes helps maintain the team's functioning by helping all members feel supported and collectively responsible for reaching predetermined goals.

Despite these potential uncomfortable feelings, the analysis of student reading data remains an essential and vital component of identifying literacy problems, understanding barriers that have kept or could keep students from reaching the goals, and monitoring the impact of instructional and intervention practices on student reading outcomes.

Selecting Student Data. An effective protocol for analyzing all available student reading data begins with first analyzing broad or general school-wide reading trends. For instance, state summative reading assessments (e.g., Florida Comprehensive Achievement Test, Texas Assessment of Knowledge and Skills) can lend critical information regarding overall effectiveness of literacy instruction as well as indicate a need for specific literacy supports. The state assessment data may reveal that students lack sufficient knowledge of vocabulary to read and comprehend grade-level text or that many students failed to respond accurately to questions that required them to analyze or synthesize information. Taking time to break down student summative data helps the team more clearly identify specific areas on which to focus.

It is important, however, to recognize the limitations of reviewing only state summative assessments. Summative data helps the team understand the general areas where student learning is breaking down. However, it does not typically provide enough information for the team to determine why students are struggling in one or more general areas. While the Reading First program describes reading as a "complex system of deriving meaning from print" that requires phonetic knowledge, the ability to decode unfamiliar words, reading fluency, sufficient background knowledge and vocabulary development, the ability to apply active reading strategies to construct meaning from print, and motivation to read (No Child Left Behind Act, 2001), most state assessments fall short of measuring all of the skills, abilities, and attitudes associated with successful adolescent readers. For instance, only 35% of state assessments explicitly measure vocabulary skills, and even fewer measure such foundational reading skills as word analysis (16%) or fluency (8%) (Johnstone et al., 2007).

Although most states include standards that likely impact students' motivation to read (e.g., personal growth through reading, reflection upon self through reading, relating text to real life), no state directly assesses these standards through the state reading assessment. Thus, teams need to ensure their assessment protocols include state reading assessments to identify which students require additional reading instruction and targeted diagnostic assessments aimed at gathering important information regarding students' foundational reading skills, knowledge of reading strategies, vocabulary development, and motivation to read (Morsy, Kieffer, & Snow, 2010). Reviewing summative assessments guides the team's inquiry but should not be the limit of the inquiry.

After reviewing state assessment results to determine general literacy trends, teams should plan to administer formal literacy assessments to evaluate students' literacy development throughout the school year and prior to the administration of the state summative assessment. Analysis of the assessment data allows teams to augment core literacy instruction as necessary throughout the school year.

Teams may also consider administering brief, informal assessments to collect valuable information beyond what is revealed through the state summative assessement or other formal literacy assessments. For example, if teams wish to collect information about which literacy skills and strategies students utilize while reading, they may wish to add a literacy process interview to their assessment protocol. In general, literacy process interviews are conducted with students who have not yet mastered grade-level reading standards as a means of identifying individual needs. Another option is to create a student survey of previously taught strategies to determine which strategies students know and are able to use. This information provides valuable information for problem analysis and intervention planning.

The value of these types of informal assessments became apparent at one of the schools in which we work. The school developed two surveys: one for students to identify strategies they used and another for teachers to identify the strategies teachers taught. The results were significant. After analyzing the data, the school determined that although teachers reported they taught strategies, students were not familiar with them and did not report that they used them. This data was then compared to the administrative walk-through data, which indicated that 90% of the time, administrators observed teachers lecturing instead of engaging students in authentic reading activities and rarely providing students with opportunities to apply previously taught strategies. This informal data led to the design of an action plan that included teacher support for providing modeled instruction and implementing small collaborative group activities to support guided practice with reading comprehension strategies.

Teams should also attempt to utilize standardized informal assessments such as Curriculum-Based Measurement (CBM) probes whenever possible to allow for more accurate summarization and interpretation of assessment results across groups of students (Fuchs & Fuchs, 2003). Collecting and analyzing these types of data throughout the year informs reading intervention planning and allows teams to make necessary changes to intervention supports for students who require more intensive reading intervention to master grade-level reading standards.

Literacy assessments range from formal, standardized assessment batteries to informal assessments, including informal reading inventories, content reading inventories, literacy process interviews, literacy attitude surveys, literacy practice interviews, and portfolios. A balanced literacy assessment protocol typically includes formal literacy assessments combined with dynamic assessments embedded throughout literacy instruction with students. Well-designed literacy plans include analysis of formal state-wide data combined with school-based assessments administered three times a year for all students and more frequently for students who require intervention to meet grade-level literacy expectations.

Teams need to carefully consider the number and types of assessments they include and the impact of these assessments on students. The negative feelings many adolescents associate with assessment forces teams to consider how to accurately and routinely assess adolescents' literacy development without spending an exessive amount of time and energy engaged in the assessment process. The key is to identify and plan for the administration of literacy assessments while taking care not to focus so entirely on the collection and analysis of student assessment data that little time, energy, and other resources are available to support data analysis, instructional planning, and targeted intervention. It is not uncommon for teams to find themselves in a cycle of "data admiration" in which new data is consistently collected and reviewed in order to determine the continued existence of a literacy problem but is never used effectively for intervention planning. The use of a problem-solving protocol with guiding questions that help guide teams through the four-step process (i.e., problem identification, problem analysis, intervention planning, and program evaluation) can prevent teams from getting stuck in the problem-identification step.

Selecting Teacher Data. The collection and analysis of teacher-level data are equal in importance to collecting and analyzing student data for improving literacy outcomes. Teacher perceptions of students' abilities to succeed, their expertise at embedding effective literacy instruction throughout curriculum, and their willingness to change instruction in response to students' needs critically impacts students' achievement. Collecting and analyzing this type of teacher data can be a bit tricky, since LLT members are collecting information from their peers. However, with careful planning and transparency about how the data will be used, teams can include teacher data as part of their comprehensive data collection plan.

One way to include teacher data is by collecting group data. Rather than collecting teacher-specific information, the team analyzes collective teacher data, such as the percentage of teachers who have attended identified professional development or implemented a specific literacy strategy. Administrators can report the percentage of classroom observations within which they observed specific instructional strategies or components on which teachers were provided training. The team can then compare the data to determine the effectiveness of the professional development and identify additional professional development that may be needed to support the full implementation of the school's literacy action plan. Administrators can use the data to determine which teachers need additional support through ongoing professional development and instructional coaching.

Keep in mind that once a plan has been developed, determining its effectiveness is dependent on the ability to determine the extent to which components of the plan were implemented with fidelity. If, for instance, the action plan includes opportunities for teachers to attend professional development focused on a particular instructional change, simply collecting attendance data at the professional development session will not provide the team with enough information to determine whether the instructional change has occurred. The team must collect additional data (e.g., classroom observation data) to determine whether the instruction has improved as a result of professional development. The team may even want to compare the student achievement data of students enrolled in classes where the instructional change has occurred with data from students who are enrolled in classes where the instructional change has not been implemented. This information will assist the team in understanding the impact of the instructional strategy on student outcomes.

The method for collecting this type of data can take on many forms. Classroom observation data can be collected and reported by an administrator or instructional coach. The team might consider developing teacher and student surveys to identify perceptions of skill development and implementation, and reviewing teacher lesson plans and minutes of professional learning community meetings where teachers gather for common planning. The key is to develop a means for collecting data to analyze the effectiveness and implementation fidelity of strategies and interventions identifed in the literacy action plan.

Identifying Instructional, Curricular, and Environmental Barriers. Identifying instructional, curricular, and environmental barriers to student literacy achievement is critical to the development of effective literacy plans. An analysis of the variables that could prevent or have prevented students from reaching expected levels allows teams to uncover and understand the root causes of literacy problems at their school. Without an understanding of the root causes of the school's literacy problems, LLTs tend to develop school-wide literacy plans that "should" work to improve student literacy but often, unfortunately, do not. Many times these plans consist of strategies that team members have heard are effective at other schools or strategies that they have seen work in other settings. It is not uncommon for teams to make the assumption that strategies that are effective at other schools will work as effectively at their own school. Unfortunately, if chosen strategies do not address the barriers that contribute to or cause the school's literacy problems, they are likely to be ineffective. Thus, teams cannot simply transplant an effective literacy plan from one school to another and expect the exact same results, unless of course the underlying instructional, curricular, and environmental barriers are the same.

It is not unusual for secondary teams to initially identify student motivation and parent involvement as the primary barriers to student literacy achievement. Teams often report a general belief that students don't care enough about learning and as result are not self-initiating or engaged in the learning process. This sentiment is intimately tied to a common belief that parents, particularly those of at-risk students, do not value education and as a result do not encourage or supervise their children's engagement or achievement at school.

Schools do not control all the reasons students become disengaged at school, and although some of these reasons are tied to the students' home and community lives, a majority of the variables that impact student engagement are directly under the control of the school. According to research completed by the National Research Council Committee on Increasing High School Students' Engagement and Motivation to Learn (2003),

> Engaging schools and teachers promote students' confidence to learn and succeed in school by providing challenging instruction and support for meeting high standards, and they clearly convey their own high expectations for student outcomes. They provide choices for students and they make the curriculum and instruction relevant to adolescents' experiences, cultures, and long-term goals, so that students see some value in the high school curriculum. (pp. 3–4)

Thus, instead of focusing on student motivation as the sole barrier to student achievement, LLTs must work to identify instructional, curricular, and environmental barriers that not only impact student motivation and engagement in the learning process but ultimately contribute to student literacy outcomes. The presence of specific instructional, curricular, and environmental conditions have been found to be significantly related to positive student literacy outcomes. The absence of these conditions may constitute barriers to student literacy development and thus should be addressed by the LLT within the school-wide literacy plan. The National Research Council's (2003) meta-analysis of existing literature on effective literacy programming revealed the following key components, which all LLTs should consider:

- ◆ Relationships with peers and adults
  - Adult-student interactions are respectful and positive.
  - Peer interactions are respectful and positive.
  - Opportunities are provided for structured peer collaboration and discourse.
- ◆ Authentic tasks
  - Reading and writing activities relate to students' outside world.
  - Tasks require application to real-world problems and settings.
  - Tasks link directly to essential objectives of lesson, and this link is explicitly made for students.
- ◆ Capitalization of cultural knowledge
  - Texts and tasks are related to students' existing background knowledge.
  - Curriculum is culturally sensitive and teaches technical literacy concepts using culturally familiar and sensitive texts and materials, including connections to students' native language or vernacular.

- Instruction provides structured opportunities for students to use both English and their native language or vernacular for learning.
◆ Use of multiple resources
  - Students are allowed to learn from peers, from materials in their native language, and from computers.
  - Students are allowed to demonstrate knowledge in multiple modalities, including writing, speaking, drawing, and performing.
◆ Rigorous and challenging instruction
  - Tasks require students to learn new constructs through reading and to express their conceptualization through writing as opposed to simply recalling facts.
  - Tasks focus on students' synthesis and expression of their ideas instead of focusing on students' ability to choose between right and wrong answers.
  - Tasks require students to apply what they have learned to novel situations.
  - Tasks require students to make connections between multiple reading sources and between the text and their own experiences.
◆ Explicit instruction
  - Explicit instruction is provided in "discipline-specific strategies for asking questions, making and testing predictions, summarizing, drawing inferences, using prior knowledge, and self-monitoring" (p. 69).
◆ Frequent feedback from assessments
  - Students are provided with frequent feedback on their progress toward mastery of reading skills and strategies.
  - Students are supported in setting and monitoring reasonable yet ambitious goals for their own reading development.
◆ Integrated curricula
  - Curricula continually link back to the essential questions/objectives of the content area across lessons and units of instruction.
  - Curricula and instruction provide explicit and integrated instruction on how, when, and why to use specific literacy strategies within different content areas.
  - Common literacy strategies are taught and reinforced school-wide.

Collecting relevant data to identify instructional, curricular, and environmental barriers becomes a starting point for understanding the cultural and instructional changes needed to improve student literacy outcomes.

Designing and Implementing Instruction and Interventions. If a literacy leadership team has taken the necessary steps to establish a highly functioning group and to carefully analyze student, teacher, and schoolwide data, then it is now ready to embark on the process of examining research to address the identified barriers, taking an important step toward achieving the school's literacy goals. A thorough analysis of the instructional, curricular, and environmental conditions that promote or impede student literacy development serves as the basis for designing literacy instruction and intervention. The link between identified barriers to student literacy and the strategies chosen to improve student literacy is paramount. For example, if it is hypothesized that students have not achieved expected literacy outcomes because curricular materials are not culturally sensitive or relevant to students, then teams might choose to focus on expanding classroom libraries to include more culturally relevant reading materials and planning lessons that incorporate these texts.

Teams should incorporate instructional and intervention strategies based on a thorough understanding of the root causes of literacy problems within their school-wide plan. Time and energy should be devoted to ensuring that strategies utilized within reading intervention classrooms (Tier 2 and Tier 3) align with Tier 1 strategies and goals. For example, if all students will be provided with explicit instruction on specific reading strategies within their English/language arts classes and guided practice with the strategies with grade-level text within their other content courses, then reading intervention classrooms should provide additional explicit instruction, modeling, and guided and independent practice with the strategies using student-accessible text.

Instructional and intervention plans should include a detailed plan to support the implementation of strategies and to monitor the fidelity of implementation. Without strong support plans, literacy strategies are unlikely to be implemented with fidelity school-wide (Gresham, MacMillan, Beebe-Frankenberger, & Bocian, 2000). LLTs should specifically articulate the goals and expected outcomes of instructional strategies teachers are expected to implement, describe the strategies in detail, provide all instructors with required materials and resources, plan and provide any necessary staff development and follow-up coaching needed by staff to implement the strategies as intended, and determine and communicate the frequency and form of fidelity checks and progress monitoring.

Evaluating the Plan

Along with planning strategies to support implementation, LLTs should also determine how the effectiveness of the intervention strategies will be

FIGURE 3.1 Positive Student Response

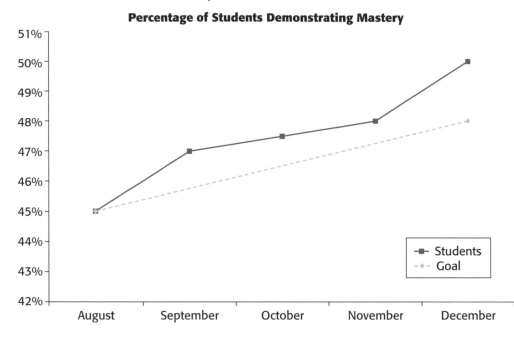

evaluated. Specifically, teams should decide what student data will need to be collected over time; who will be responsible for collecting, managing, and analyzing the student-outcome data; how often the data will be reviewed; and what will be considered a positive result prior to implementing the literacy plan.

It is important for LLTs to base instructional decisions on student outcome data and not on individuals' opinions as to whether the strategies are having the desired effect or are worth the required effort to implement. Individuals' perceptions regarding the impact of strategies on students' reading growth are rarely sensitive enough to detect incremental growth over short periods of time. For instance, a teacher is unlikely to perceive any difference between a student who can read 92 words correctly in a one-minute period one week and 96 words correctly the following week, although a gain of four words read correctly in a one-week period is fairly significant. Detecting such incremental change most often requires the administration of an oral reading fluency probe and analysis of the resulting data.

Effectiveness of literacy plans should be determined by comparing the rate of student progress to the rate of progress required to close the current level–expected level gap within the specified time period. Data that indicates that the rate of progress is sufficient to close the gap between the current levels and the expected levels within the specified time period represents a positive response to the literacy plans. Positive responses should be celebrated,

FIGURE 3.2 Insufficient Student Response

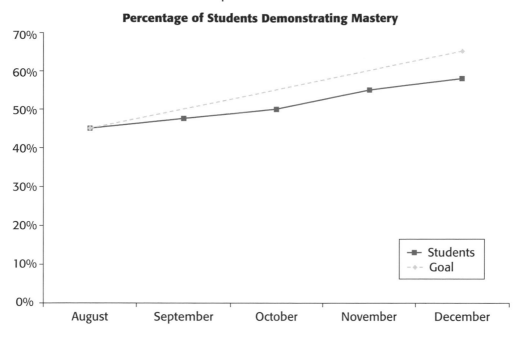

Percentage of Students Demonstrating Mastery

and a literacy plan that results in a positive student response should be continued until the current level–expected level gap is completely eliminated (see Figure 3.1: Positive Student Response).

Data that indicates students are improving but not at a rate sufficient to close the current level–expected level gap in the specified time frame represents an insufficient student response to the literacy plan (see Figure 3.2: Insufficient Student Response). Insufficient student response patterns indicate that while the literacy plan is having a positive effect on student literacy, the impact is not significant enough to achieve the literacy goal within the specified time period. This type of response suggests that the LLT likely chose the right strategies to address the underlying barriers to student literacy. However, the insufficient response also indicates that the intensity of the strategies needs to be increased in order to increase the rate of student response. The intensification of strategies can be achieved by doing the following:

◆ Increasing time and response opportunities
◆ Improving core program efficacy
◆ Improving core program implementation
◆ Decreasing group size
◆ Increasing coordination of programming and instruction (Simmons, Kameenui, Stoolmiller, Coyne, and Harn, 2003)

FIGURE 3.3 Poor Student Response

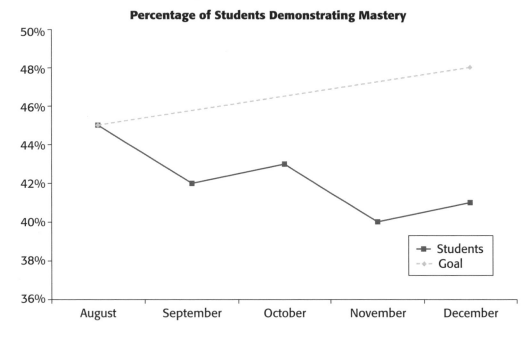

Data indicating that the gap between the current literacy level and the expected literacy level is either maintaining or becoming wider over time indicates a poor student response to the literacy plan (see Figure 3.3: Poor Student Response). When a poor student response occurs, LLTs should first examine the fidelity of implementation. Literacy strategies that are not implemented with fidelity are unlikely to have positive impact on student literacy outcomes. If the LLT determines that the literacy plan was not implemented with fidelity, the team should problem solve the fidelity issue in order to determine the barriers to implementation and develop a plan to address the identified barriers and thus improve fidelity. If the LLT determines that the literacy plan was implemented as intended but nonethelesss resulted in a poor student response, LLTs should cycle back to the problem-analysis phase of the problem-solving process in order to determine if alternative barriers should be addressed within the literacy plan.

Conclusion

Literacy leadership teams are powerful change agents when implemented correctly. They have the power to change the culture of schools through careful analysis of data and research on and support of effective instruction.

Successful teams identify concerns, analyze school-wide data, review research-based strategies leading to improving student achievement, develop action plans to address the concerns, and provide ongoing support for teachers to enable them to implement the changes with fidelity. More important, they utilize the problem-solving/response-to-intervention framework to guide their work and inform their decisions.

The remaining chapters specifically discuss research-based suggestions for addressing student engagement, intensifying and improving literacy instruction, planning for tiered intervention supports, and providing teachers with the support they need to fully engage in the school-wide literacy plans.

4

Addressing Student Engagement and Motivation Issues

When educators believe that motivation lies entirely within individual stu-
dents, there is no incentive to alter the motivational structure of the school
or classroom. . . . Educators can directly enhance student motivation by
altering controllable factors such as teaching style, curricula, and school
or classroom policies. Conversely, this view holds educators more account-
able for motivating students. Stated differently, if the student could be more
motivated if the environmental conditions were right, then educators must
assume some personal responsibility for the student's motivation and, by
extension, for the student's apparent lack of motivation.
—Urdan & Schoenfelder, 2006, p. 345

Not long ago, an English teacher working in a struggling school requested
digital readers as opposed to paperback books for her students. The principal
responded that he didn't quite understand why the school should invest in
digital readers because the only thing they might impact is student motivation. Hmmmm . . .

The irony in this story is that educators cite a lack of student motivation
to read as the primary reason for underachievement in reading as well as a
significant barrier for student mastery of academic standards (Strommen &
Mates, 2004). Motivating adolescents to read, particularly those who struggle
to meet grade-level reading expectations, is a significant challenge for educators. By the time students reach middle school, adolescents' motivation to
read lags well below that of elementary students. In fact, few adolescents
choose to read on their own (Pitcher, Albright, Delaney, et. al, 2007) with
fewer than 30% of adolescents reporting reading daily for enjoyment (Dreher,

2003). Surprisingly, even competent readers often report they hate to read (Worthy, 1998). Struggling readers spend significantly less time than their more competent peers engaged in reading, resulting in a discrepancy of more than one million more words independently read by more competent readers each year (Cunningham & Stanovich, 2003). This huge discrepancy no doubt significantly contributes to the ever-expanding gap between the reading skills of more- and less-competent readers. Recognizing the reluctance of adolescents to choose to read for pleasure or for learning, schools must create systems that encourage and engage students in the reading process. Addressing student motivation to read and engage in the reading process is a necessary step in addressing student achievement for adolescents.

Reading and Achievement

It is most unfortunate that so many adolescents express reluctance to read because reading engagement is highly correlated to reading achievement. In fact, time spent engaged in reading is the strongest predictor of reading achievement (Kirsch et al., 2002). Further, high rates of reading engagement can help students overcome significant risk factors for reading underachievement, including those associated with low family income and educational history. Research has shown that highly engaged readers from low-income/low-education families typically outperform less-engaged readers from high-income/high-education families (Guthrie, Shafer, & Huang, 2001). Studies focusing on lowering the achievement gap between high-performing and low-performing students emphasize the importance of reflecting on the impact of motivation and engagement on student achievement (Guthrie et al., 2004), especially for high school students who often have many years of struggle and failure to overcome. Even students who did not experience reading difficulties during their elementary years become less motivated and engaged in reading as they move from elementary to middle to high school (Guthrie, 2001). Hence, it becomes increasingly important as students progress through the educational system to implement strategies and supports that improve student motivation and reading engagement as a means of improving student achievement.

Teacher Beliefs

While the majority of teachers value motivation as an integral component of reading achievement (Gambrell, 1996), many believe that motivating students to engage in literacy activities is beyond their influence or perhaps even beyond their professional responsibility. Many teachers do not fully understand the impact of instructional, curricular, and environmental variables over which they have significant influence on student motivation and engagement levels. A survey of 614 reading and language arts teachers at Florida's low-performing high schools revealed that 43% of responding teachers did not believe they possessed the necessary skills to motivate students to engage in learning (Craig, 2006). These same teachers were confident of their ability to teach their content (92%) and to manage the classroom (94%). Yet even with these skill sets, many of these same teachers felt powerless to engage students in learning.

Professional development linking teachers' instructional behaviors and students' attitudes toward learning is often needed to empower teachers to incorporate strategies that help improve student motivation and engagement (Turner & Patrick, 2004). Without such training, teacher preconceptions about variables that impact student motivation and engagement (e.g., student attitude, family influences) can impede successful implementation of instructional changes needed to improve student outcomes. For instance, Thompson, Warren, and Carter (2004) surveyed 121 high school teachers in Southern California and found "nearly 60 percent of the participants blamed students for their underachievement" (p. 11). Essentially, while many teachers are confident in their ability to teach their content and manage student behavior, they often feel helpless to impact student engagement levels and underachievement. As a result, these teachers are unlikely to implement recommended instructional strategies with fidelity.

For teachers in low-performing schools or classrooms, placing blame for low student achievement on student motivation and engagement allows teachers to maintain their own sense of efficacy as effective teachers by arguing that student performance is directly related to student motivation, over which they have little or no control. Unfortunately, this way of thinking leads to a belief that changes to the instruction, curriculum, or environment will have little or no impact on students' motivation, engagement, or outcomes. When teachers believe that student motivation is the result of influences related to learner and family variables, which are beyond their control, it reinforces their belief that they are not responsible for motivating students, engaging them in the learning process, or improving student achievement. Consequently, the responsibility for improving student achievement is firmly placed on the student rather than on instruction.

Teachers' beliefs about their ability to impact student motivation, engagement, and learning can often serve to impede or expand school-based restructuring. Teachers who believe they can positively impact students' learning produce higher student achievement than those who believe their students are incapable of success (Langer, 2001). These teachers are less likely to blame students for low performance and are more likely to reexamine their own teaching as a means of improving student achievement (Hall, Hines, Bacon, & Koulianos, 1992). The most effective teachers recognize their ability to "enhance student motivation by altering controllable factors such as teaching style, curricula, and school or classroom policies" (Urdan & Schoenfelder, 2006, p. 345) and as a result are more likely to take the necessary steps to change the classroom environment. Literacy leadership teams (LLTs) must work collaboratively to identify ways to reinforce teachers' beliefs that their students can learn when provided with changes in instructional delivery.

One School's Example. Collecting school-based data is one way to shift the focus away from placing blame toward solving problems. One alternative middle school in a large metropolitan area, faced with growing concerns about student achievement, spent considerable time focusing on student behaviors that teachers believed hindered student learning. At the time, many teachers expressed a belief that students' lack of achievement resulted from students' general lack of caring about school and parents' general lack of supervision and guidance regarding the importance of school. When asked what made them think that students and their parents did not "care" about school, teachers relayed that many or most students came to school or class unprepared. After some discussion, the team defined "prepared" as arriving to class with completed homework assignments and having all the necessary materials for class (e.g., textbooks, pencils, paper). The reading coach persuaded the LLT to examine the hypothesis by collecting data. Teachers spent two weeks collecting data to determine how many students turned in homework and came to school with supplies and materials. Much to the teachers' surprise, a large majority (more than 70%) of their students met their definition of "prepared" (i.e., turned in homework and came to class with necessary materials). The teachers were even more surprised to find that the percentage of students who turned in assignments correlated with the percentage of teachers who turned in their data for analysis. Data collection and analysis allowed teachers to shift their focus away from internal student attributes and move toward examining variables that impacted student motivation and engagement over which they had more influence (i.e., instruction, curriculum, and environmental variables), thus beginning the problem-solving process.

Improving Student Motivation and Reading Engagement

As with the example provided, LLTs should examine instructional, curricular, and environmental barriers that negatively impact student motivation and

engagement in literacy activities and help teachers understand the relationship between these barriers and student reading achievement. Strategies that
remove or lessen the impact of instructional, curricular, and environmental
barriers on student motivation should be considered central to any school-
wide literacy plan.

Cambourne (1995) contends that engagement is the result of multiple personal attributes that include identifying a purpose for learning, possessing a
desire to understand, believing in one's own ability to learn the material, and
taking personal responsibility for the learning. Implementing strategies and
supports at school that help students understand the purpose for reading,
foster their curiosity, improve their reading confidence, and provide them
with a sense of ownership will improve students' reading engagement, leading to increased reading achievement. Instructional, curricular, and environmental barriers that negatively impact student motivation and engagement
in reading can be removed through the application of specific strategies and
supports. Strategies and supports to maximize student engagement should
be incorporated into the LLT's literacy plan.

Instructional Drivers and Barriers

Fostering Students' Authentic Engagement. The traditional "teacher lectures,
students listen" mode of instruction, which still dominates many secondary
classrooms, is related to lower student motivation, engagement, and reading
achievement than more active and authentic learning opportunities. According to research completed by Marks (2000), students consider schoolwork to
be interesting and engaging when it is

- ◆ active and experiential in nature;
- ◆ varied rather than repetitive;
- ◆ meaningful and linked to life outside school;
- ◆ challenging, providing opportunity for sustained thinking and
  exploration, without being too difficult;
- ◆ individualized, recognizing that students differ from one another in
  needs, capacities and perspectives;
- ◆ designed to involve them in making decisions about the planning,
  implementing, reporting and assessing of work, allowing some
  autonomy and control;
- ◆ designed to include talking and working with other students.

Students' perspective on engaging schoolwork is consistent with what is
known about how people, in general, learn most effectively. Strong conceptual

understanding rarely occurs when the learning process is not active and is enhanced when instruction allows for interaction with others, exploration and interpretation of ideas, and real-world, relevant application. Authentic engagement of students relies on "authentic pedagogy," which Newman, Marks, & Gamoran (1995) describe as instructional practices that include construction of knowledge, disciplined inquiry, and value beyond the school.

The first step in construction of knowledge is to acknowledge students' existing understanding and experience. Understanding students' prior knowledge and pre- or misconceptions is critical to the learning process. According to Donovan & Bransford (2005), "If students' preconceptions are not addressed directly, they often memorize content (e.g., formulas in physics), yet still use their experience-based preconceptions to act in the world" (p. 5). Beginning lessons by activating prior knowledge also helps engage students in the learning process by sending the message that they are already competent in the subject matter. Feelings of competency are significantly related to student engagement levels. Students who feel more competent within a subject area are more likely to engage in the learning process than are students who believe they lack critical background knowledge and competencies (Christenson et al., 2008).

Second, designing classroom activities that facilitate student inquiry is essential to students' construction of knowledge and deepening conceptual understanding (Marzano, 2003). Structured inquiry activities allow students to build on their prior knowledge while developing a deeper understanding through the integration and application of new information.

The third criterion for authentic pedagogy is value beyond school. Students perceive value beyond the school when they can connect the content to personal or social issues as well as demonstrate their understanding to an audience outside the classroom or school (Newman, Marks, & Gamoran, 1995). Providing students with opportunities to link instruction to real-life experiences expands their willingness to engage in learning activities.

Teachers must incorporate instructional practices and delivery models that allow time for students to make connections between their own lives and the content they are expected to learn as well as time to discuss and analyze the misperceptions that inhibit their understanding. Incorporating opportunities for students to express their own ideas and connect their ideas to the content aids in the development of a conceptual understanding of the information provided through instruction. As students begin to experience validation of their own experiences, they are more likely to engage in the learning process and find ways to incorporate new information into their learning schema.

Explicit, Modeled, and Guided Strategy Instruction. Unfortunately, instruction within many secondary classrooms comprises primarily lecture followed by long periods of independent seat work (e.g., work sheets or silent reading). Oftentimes, lecture within reading classrooms centers around "telling" students rather than "teaching" them. For instance, we have observed that in many reading intervention classrooms, teachers have a tendency to tell students the definition of author's purpose (e.g., the reason the author wrote the text) rather than explicitly teaching the students strategies for determining the author's purpose (e.g., review the text title, determine the ratio of facts to opinions within the text, etc.). This type of instruction serves only to reinforce that determining the author's purpose is important without providing students with the ability to be successful with the task. Students within these classrooms are likely to report feeling bored, frustrated, and unmotivated.

Even worse, far too many secondary teachers simply assign reading activities and then assess the students' progress without providing students with explicit instruction followed by opportunities to practice. These classrooms often emphasize assigning grades rather than improving student reading outcomes. Because little or no instruction is provided to students, student reading achievement within these classrooms rarely improves, and students are likely to receive a failing grade in the course, serving only to reinforce students' low confidence in their reading ability.

We have also noted in our review of grades assigned to students in reading intervention classes at several of Florida's lowest-performing schools that 30% to 75% of students enrolled in reading intervention courses received either an F or a D for their final grade. Interviews with reading intervention teachers from these schools revealed that the teachers often felt they had "no choice" in assigning students low or failing grades because many students failed to complete assignments or engage in classroom activities. Students from these schools report poor or nonexistent relationships with teachers, "boring" instruction, and feelings of hopelessness that they will ever read on grade level as the reason for their disengagement.

Providing students with explicit, modeled, and guided strategy instruction and then focusing on monitoring and reinforcing students' application of strategies gives the support and feedback that students need to stay engaged in the learning process (Archer & Hughes, 2011; Carnegie Council on Advancing Adolescent Literacy, 2010; Fisher & Frey, 2008; Schmoker, 2011). In this scenario, students receive explicit instruction on how and when to utilize a particular reading strategy. Explicit instruction is followed by modeled instruction during which the teacher demonstrates the use of the reading strategy to better understand the text and/or answer a reading comprehension question. The main goal of the modeled instruction phase is to provide students with a model of not only the application of the strategy but also the internal self-talk associated with selecting and using the strategy to complete an academic task. Guided practice follows, which includes scaf-folded teacher and/or peer support for students while they practice using the strategy themselves. The students are provided with positive and correc-tive feedback throughout the guided-practice phase. If students are unable to apply the strategy successfully, the teacher moves back to explicit or mod-eled instruction to reteach the strategy and then allows the students another opportunity to practice the strategy with support. Once the students are able to apply the strategy effectively, the teacher assigns some independent prac-tice within which the students are expected to apply the strategy to complete an academic task without teacher or peer support. Students who are unable to effectively apply the strategy independently should not be assigned a fail-ing grade but should be provided with more explicit, modeled, or guided practice.

This type of instructional approach increases the likelihood that students will receive the amount of support, instruction, feedback, and practice needed to remain engaged in the learning process and master important reading strategies. Further, students who are taught why, how, and when to use spe-cific reading strategies feel more competent and confident in their ability to learn from text (Hogan and Pressley, 1997), and more confident readers are typically more motivated to engage in reading (Guthrie & Wigfield, 2000).

Structured Peer Collaboration. Providing students with the opportunity to share their reading experiences with peers increases student engagement and improves student achievement (Langer, Close, Angelis, & Preller, 2000). It is important to note, however, that simply providing students with the oppor-tunity to work together without providing structure and accountability for each member may not result in improved student reading outcomes. Provid-ing structure to student collaborative work, such as assigning each member an important role (e.g., recorder, spokesperson, or researcher who accesses and reports information for the group), helps groups be more productive and focused. Collaborative group work should focus on facilitating students' thoughtful, reflective discussion through the promotion of high-level ques-tioning and conversation.

A balanced literacy program should include frequent opportunities for students to engage in structured group work. Structured collaborative activities, such as literacy circles, can provide social motivation for students to engage in reading. In literature circles, small groups of students gather together to discuss a piece of literature in depth. The students guide the discussion and their interpretation and opinion of what they have read. Dis-cussions often include analysis of events and characters in the book, the author's purpose and style, and students' personal experiences related to the story. Literature circles provide opportunities for students to engage in critical thinking and reflection as they read, discuss, and respond to books. Further, the students' collaboration allows them to reshape and add to their understanding as they construct meaning with other readers through structured discussion and common writing assignments (Noe & Johnson, 1999). This type of literacy activity provides students with social motivation to read and "leads to increased amount of reading and high achievement in reading" (Guthrie & Wigfield, 2000, p. 408).

Curricular Drivers and Barriers

Offering Choice and Autonomy. Another important factor in facilitating student engagement is giving students the power to choose their own reading materials (Pitcher et al., 2007). Allowing students a choice of supplemental books and other reading materials positively impacts students' engagement and reading comprehension (Biancarosa & Snow, 2004). Empowering students to make decisions about topics and selections of materials fosters greater student ownership and responsibility for their engagement in learning (Guthrie & Humenick, 2004). Although individual teachers may feel they are limited in their ability to provide students with supplemental materials, working with and through the LLT to incorporate strategies that allow students the opportunity to choose texts and topics is worth the effort, as it results in greater student ownership for learning and higher rates of engagement.

Providing Relevant and Interesting Literacy Materials and Activities. Teachers who have a thorough understanding of students' interests, personal goals, and experiences more easily select topics that are relevant and interesting to their students (Guthrie, Wigfield, & VonSecker, 2000). Utilizing reading material that relates to what the students are learning in other classes can also help students see the importance of reading and engaging in literacy activities. For instance, students who are provided with explicit instruction in vocabulary related to their science class and who engage in guided reading with their science text will not only be actively engaged in important literacy activities but will also likely perform more successfully in their science classroom. The connection between reading content materials and performing more successfully not only in reading but also in content classes will help students to see the relevancy of reading to their overall academic success.

While reading teachers are likely to find more success motivating their students by incorporating content area text and supplemental reading materials, content teachers should also reinforce this effort by explicitly incorporating reading strategies common to those taught within reading classrooms. Students will be more motivated to learn and utilize reading strategies when they understand how the strategies can be effectively employed in multiple classes than if reading strategies are perceived as being related only to reading in reading classes or for state reading assessments (Kamil et al., 2008).

Environmental Barriers

The learning environment plays a critical and significant role in motivating and engaging students in literacy activities. The quality of the relationships between students and teachers serves as a foundation for student success. A positive and supportive relationship between teacher and students fosters student motivation and engagement (Fenzel & O'Brennan, 2007) and ultimately improves reading achievement. Teachers who spend time understanding the unique needs and interests of their students and take the time to show students that they are interested in and care about them will likely have students who are motivated and engaged in the learning process (Parris & Collins Block, 2007).

Classrooms within which teachers clearly and consistently communicate classroom norms and procedures are also associated with higher student engagement rates. Students often report feeling more secure in classrooms where behavioral and academic expectations are clearly established and fairly and consistently applied than in classrooms where expectations are unclear or inconsistently applied. Peer norms and values are also an important aspect of the classroom environment. Teachers can help establish positive peer relationships when they encourage and enforce positive peer-to-peer interactions. As such, teachers should avoid making public comparisons of students' work, putting students or classes down, or showing preference for higher-performing students.

Constructing classroom environments that are task-oriented rather than performance-oriented also leads to higher student motivation and engagement rates (Fenzel & O'Brennan, 2007). See Figure 4.1: Learning Environments (page 68) for a comparison of task-oriented and performance-oriented classrooms. While performance-oriented classrooms emphasize student progress in relation to others, task-oriented classrooms focus on increasing effort and individual improvement. Assisting students in setting goals focusing on improving their personal effort (e.g., time spent reading independently) and their individual reading outcomes (e.g., increasing their oral reading fluency rate) and then tailoring instruction to assist students in reaching their goals will improve student buy-in to instruction and provide more immediate and positive reinforcement

FIGURE 4.1 Learning Environments

Performance-Oriented Learning Environments	*Task-Oriented Learning Environments*
• Emphasis is on the importance of grades, tests, scores, and social comparisons. • Students are grouped homogenously by ability. • Pull-out and retention programs are used. • Instruction and assessment emphasize correct answers over understanding.	• Emphasis is on effort, mastery, and improvement. • Mixed-ability classrooms are used. • Cross-age and peer tutoring programs are used. • Time is used flexibly to allow strategic and short-term grouping. • Student mistakes are regarded as integral to learning.

Anderman, Maehr, & Midgley, 1999; Haselhuhn, Al-Mabuk, Gabriele, Groen, & Galloway, 2007

for students' personal goal attainment. In contrast, classrooms in which grades, test scores, and student progress are emphasized in relation to other students are likely to disenfranchise students whose reading achievement has been well below that of their peers for several years. Virtually all struggling readers are painfully aware of their reading achievement compared to their more successful peers. Emphasizing these differences only serves to disempower students regarding their ability to improve their own reading achievement levels.

Learner Barriers

Student Confidence. Students' perception of their own ability to read and write impacts their motivation to learn and engagement in the learning process (Alvermann, 2001). Students who believe they are incapable of succeeding are less motivated to engage in activities that promote learning. As such, students who perceive themselves to be capable readers are more likely to persist in reading difficult texts, exert extra effort when they do not initially understand what is written, and assimilate what is read with their prior knowledge than their less confident peers (Guthrie & Wigfield, 2000). Thus, helping students feel academically confident and capable is critically important to improving student academic outcomes.

As students grow older, their capacity to understand their own reading performance, as well as the feedback they receive regarding their reading ability, impacts their feelings of confidence and competency. Unfortunately, for struggling readers, this increased understanding leads to a realization that they are not as competent as others (Guthrie & Wigfield, 2000). Instructional environments that focus on social comparison between children and competition can further decrease students' reading confidence and their motivation to read (Eccles, Wigfield, & Schiefele, 1998). Instead, teachers should strive to create safe learning environments where students can track their own progress and experience personal success and growth.

Goal Setting. Students' motivation and engagement can be positively impacted by setting short-term, achievable goals and then providing classroom pacing and instruction that allows students to achieve those goals (Turner & Patrick, 2004). Students are likely to sustain their effort to achieve goals set by their teachers and even more likely to work toward goals they have set for themselves (Kamil et al., 2008). Engaging students in regular data chats is one way teachers can help students set reasonable goals and problem solve barriers to their success. The purpose of a data chat should extend beyond informing the student of his or her current reading level and focus instead on the specific strategies that will assist the student in achieving set goals as well as the progress-monitoring data that will be used to determine if the strategies are working. For instance, if a student is struggling with fluently reading grade-level text, the teacher might create fluency centers and/or activities designed to help students improve their fluency scores. Sharing with students the expected outcomes of the prescribed instructional practice on their reading achievement helps students understand the purpose for instruction, assists them in setting ambitious yet reasonable goals, and motivates students to fully engage in the instruction.

Conclusion

Student motivation and engagement is highly correlated to student reading achievement. Specific instructional, curricular, and environmental variables that include opportunities for students to set and monitor achievement goals, engage in hands-on activities, exercise choice and autonomy, access interesting and relevant texts, and collaborate with peers positively impact student motivation and engagement, which results in improved reading achievement (Guthrie et al., 2004). This is particularly true for historically low-performing students who have a tendency to become less and less engaged as they reach adolescence due to years of academic struggle and failure. Therefore, LLTs should work to include within the school's literacy plan instructional strategies combined with curricular and environmental supports that are known to positively impact student motivation and engagement in the learning process.

5

Literacy Instruction

The major message is simple—what teachers do matters . . . the greatest source of variance in our system relates to teachers.

—John Hattie, 2009

As we begin the process of determining the most effective plan to address the literacy needs of students, we urge literacy leadership teams (LLTs) to engage in the problem-solving process (e.g., problem identification, problem analysis, instruction/intervention, and program evaluation). As indicated throughout the previous chapters, we also remind schools that effective literacy initiatives must address, first and foremost, cross content literacy instruction combined with targeted intervention for students whose literacy skills are below grade level. Schools that focus all their attention and resources on remediation alone while neglecting core instruction are unlikely to realize significant and sustained improvement in student literacy achievement.

Overcoming Traditional Barriers

We begin with a brief overview of research on successful schools that have overcome traditional barriers to student success, reversed downward-trending literacy outcomes, and become highly successful schools. Often referred to as "90/90/90" schools, these schools report student success rates of 90% while serving student populations who are largely eligible for free and reduced lunch (90%) and who belong to ethnic minorities (90%) (Reeves, 2003). Reeves collected data from more than 130,000 students in 228 90/90/90 schools over four years and identified five common characteristics that contributed to their success:

- ◆ Focus on academic achievement
- ◆ Clear curriculum choices
- ◆ Frequent assessment of student progress and multiple opportunities for improvement
- ◆ Emphasis on nonfiction writing
- ◆ Collaborative scoring of student work (p. 3)

These common characteristics were critical to the success of the 90/90/90 schools and are often absent within less-successful schools that serve similar high-risk populations. Schools in high-risk communities often struggle to meet the academic needs of their students who regularly enter school with low skill levels and/or significant skill gaps, limited academic background knowledge, and insufficient vocabulary development. In addition, students from high-risk communities may also experience insufficient or unstable resources in the form of family income, housing, and health care, which may negatively impact their engagement with increasingly demanding and complex literacy expectations (National Research Council Committee on Increasing High School Students' Motivation to Learn, 2003). Addressing the nonacademic needs of students becomes paramount to improving student achievement and must be addressed within the school-wide plan.

The National Research Council Committee on Increasing High School Students' Engagement and Motivation to Learn (2004) outlined three comprehensive literacy programs (the Coalition Campus Schools Project, the Strategic Literacy Project, and the School Achievement Structure) found to be highly effective with at-risk student populations. Although each approach to literacy instruction included unique features, the overlap between the instructional approaches is considerable and should serve as the basis for every school's core literacy programming. Key features included the following:

- ◆ A focus on developing and maintaining strong personal relationships between teachers and students
- ◆ Rigorous, authentic tasks and assignments
- ◆ Explicit comprehension strategy instruction applied across multiple content areas
- ◆ Frequent formative assessment designed to provide timely feedback to teachers and students regarding student literacy progress and needs
- ◆ Culturally relevant, high-interest text and materials
- ◆ Explicit instruction to build students' background knowledge, vocabulary, and knowledge of text structures

♦ Differentiation of instruction to address individual student needs within core instruction and supplemental literacy intervention for students who require more time and practice to master grade-level standards

The research clearly reveals that successful schools develop multifaceted action plans that address individual student needs while maintaining a laser-like focus on improving student achievement. Students are expected to engage in rigorous academic tasks and are closely monitored not only to determine their success but also to modify instruction to meet individual student needs. Teachers work collaboratively to analyze student data to ensure that students are provided with the background knowledge, vocabulary development, and explicit comprehension instruction necessary to develop students' literacy skills. Essentially, all members of the school community work collaboratively to address both the academic (e.g., literacy) and nonacademic (e.g., mentoring, safety) needs of all students.

Focusing on Student Learning Goals

In our work with schools, we have found that successful schools begin with a thorough and comprehensive understanding of state standards and create action plans designed to improve student achievement relative to those standards through implementation of a multitiered system of support. Basically, successful schools begin with the end in mind (i.e., mastery of standards) and develop both short- and long-term goals based on expected student learning outcomes.

The concept of beginning with the "end in mind" is not particularly new. Stephen Covey lists it as Habit #2 of *The 7 Habits of Highly Effective People* (1989). Wiggins and McTighe (2005) promote the concept of designing curriculum based on a "backward design" model that allows teachers to identify the specific standards that students need to master and develop instruction based on the expected student outcomes. Both educators and students are more likely to achieve learning objectives when time is taken to clearly articulate and understand the goals (Naisbitt & Aburdene, 1985). Thus, it is not surprising that the problem-solving process begins by defining the "end in mind" (i.e., expected levels of performance). Schools that set clearly defined goals and expectations and focus on supporting students' achievement of those goals through the delivery of effective, research-based instruction and multitiered supports will be more likely to yield improved student achievement than schools that begin their planning process with vague or undefined goals and expectations.

Having said that, we recognize that some schools adopt a "backward design" model focusing on *what* information students should know instead of focusing on the *skills* students need to develop in order to demonstrate mastery of the standards. For instance, traditional language arts instruction at the high school level tends to focus on covering specific literary content at different grade levels. Ninth-grade students customarily are expected to read *Romeo and Juliet.* Tenth-grade students focus on world literature, while 11th-grade students focus on American literature, and 12th-grade students focus on British literature. Teachers tend to present the literature chronologically to develop a link between the literature and its reflection of culture over time. Under this model, teachers begin with the text in mind rather than student mastery of standards in mind.

A more effective approach is to begin with the standards. Instead of teachers asking, "Which texts do I need to cover?" teachers should ask, "What do my students need to know, understand, and be able to do in order to demonstrate mastery of the standards?" If we continue with the English/language arts example, instead of designing curriculum maps and pacing calendars based on predetermined texts to be covered, instruction is focused on the standards students must achieve. Texts are selected and utilized as materials necessary to teach the standards.

Consider this—if the goal of the unit is to prepare students to "analyze how an author's choices concerning how to structure a text, order events within it (e.g., parallel plots), and manipulate time (e.g., pacing, flashbacks) create such effects as mystery, tension, or surprise" (Common Core Standards Initiative, 2010, p. 38), then appropriate text is identified by whether it includes specific structures that allow students to practice the necessary strategies and develop the required skills. Instruction might begin with a short piece of text that allows the teacher to explicitly teach strategies for analyzing author's choice and identifying text structures. The teacher then models how to use the strategies to identify the specific structures used by the author, culminating with modeling how to write a summary paragraph demonstrating understanding of the skill as it is applied to the specific text. Subsequent instruction focuses on increasingly complex text, allowing students to apply the same strategies with scaffolded support.

Teachers are not the only ones in the classroom who need to have a clear understanding of the "end in mind." Throughout instruction, students need to be constantly reminded of the expected outcome. Although teachers most often have specific goals for lessons and learning activities, these goals are frequently not communicated clearly to students. As a result, learning activities can appear disjointed or unimportant. By articulating specifically what the students are expected to learn as a result of the lesson and how each learning activity is related to the learning objective, students can understand the importance of engaging in the learning process.

In addition to providing information regarding the lesson objectives, teachers should also provide information specific to the criteria for completing high-quality work. Two effective methods for clearly communicating the criteria for completing high-quality work include the use of exemplars, which show a graduation of quality up to the desired level, and rubrics, which detail each task/component expectation.

The clearer the objectives, the more motivated students will be to engage in the learning process, produce high-quality work, and achieve the learning goals. Focusing on expected student outcomes benefits both teachers and students and is more likely to lead to student success.

Unpacking the Standards

A review of English/language arts standards across states as well as the new *Common Core State Standards for English Language Arts & Literacy in History/ Social Studies, Science, & Technical Subjects* (2010), which have been adopted by most states, suggests that the focus of instruction should be placed on the skills students need in order to become more literate, not just in their language arts or reading classrooms, but within all subject areas. The goals of the *Common Core State Standards for English Language Arts & Literacy in History/ Social Studies, Science, & Technical Subjects* include developing literate adults who are capable of reading, writing, speaking, listening, and using language effectively in a variety of content areas. In order to accomplish these goals, schools must spend significant time unpacking the standards to allow teachers opportunities to clearly understand the global literacy goals and content-specific literacy goals contained in the standards. This time should also be utilized to help teachers develop an understanding of the impact of instruction and instructional strategies on student success in meeting literacy goals within and across all content areas.

Ainsworth (2003) suggests that unwrapping the standards provides "clarity as to what students must know and be able to do . . . [resulting in] more effective instructional planning, assessment, and student learning" (p. 1). The likelihood students will receive rigorous instruction that allows them to master grade-level literacy standards increases when all educators have a thorough understanding of the core grade-level standards. The effectiveness of all other strategies, including the development and use of curriculum maps, horizontally and vertically aligned assignments and activities, and common formative assessments is dependent on a thorough understanding of state standards. The process of unpacking the standards allows schools to develop comprehensive action plans that target curriculum, instruction, and assessment on specific student learning outcomes. Specifically, Ainsworth (2003) contends that unpacking the standards does the following:

♦ Improves clarity of all teachers and administrators regarding what students are expected to know, understand, and do as a result of instruction
♦ Improves horizontal and vertical alignment
♦ Improves continuity for students between courses and between grades
♦ Increases opportunities for curriculum integration
♦ Provides educators with a starting point for lesson planning and differentiated instruction
♦ Allows teachers and administrators to set instructional priorities and plan accordingly (i.e., pacing, assessment, Power Standards)

Unpacking the standards builds on traditional lesson planning objectives:

♦ What do students need to know?
♦ What do they need to understand in order to use the information independently?
♦ What do we want them to be able to do once they learn the information?

We recommend that content teams work collaboratively to review and unpack their standards as a means of developing effective lessons. Teachers who thoroughly understand expected student outcomes are more likely to engage their students in authentic tasks and activities leading to improved student achievement.

From Telling to Teaching

It is not uncommon to find teachers focusing on "main idea" as a common standard beginning in kindergarten and continuing on through high school. However, rarely do we see teachers providing direct, explicit instruction and modeling strategies to help students understand how to find the main idea in increasingly complex texts across grade levels. Unfortunately, most often we observe teachers teaching *what* the main idea is without developing students' understanding of *how* to determine the main idea, why main idea is an important concept, or how understanding main idea helps them become more effective learners.

Let's look at an example from the *Common Core State Standards for English/ Language Arts* Grade 6. Standard 2 maintains that students should be able to "determine central ideas or themes of a text and analyze their development; summarize the key supporting details and ideas" (p. 35). Basically, students are expected to be able to identify the main idea (theme) of a text and analyze how it is developed using specific supporting details and ideas found in the text. By the time students reach grades 9 and 10, the associated main idea standard becomes even more complex, requiring students to "determine a theme or central idea of a text and analyze in detail its development over the course of the text, including how it emerges and is shaped and refined by specific details; provide an objective summary of the text" (p. 38). As the complexity of the benchmark increases, so must the rigor of instruction increase to include tasks, discussions, and assessments reflective of the expected standard's cognitive complexity level.

Simply teaching students what a main idea and/or theme is from year to year will not help students develop the more complex skills of analysis necessary to master this specific standard across grade levels. The practice of unpacking the standards allows teachers time not only to understand what the standard says but also to identify specific skills students need in order to master the standard. With this information, teachers can more effectively select and implement specific instructional practices designed to promote the development of skills necessary to master the standard. The practice of unpacking standards is best completed as a collaborative process between course-alike teachers and instructional coaches. We strongly suggest that schools provide time for unpacking standards and collaborative lesson planning facilitated by instructional coaches to ensure that teachers have the support to develop instructional plans aligned to literacy standards.

Designing Instruction

How and what teachers teach significantly influences both student engagement and student achievement (National Research Council, 2004). Therefore, LLTs need to examine effective literacy instruction and its impact on student achievement as the primary focus for school improvement. Student learning improves when all teachers embed literacy instruction into their content area curriculum and support all students to successfully read required text with comprehension (Langer, 2001). For this to occur, teachers must provide students with the appropriate background knowledge and literacy strategies needed for students to engage in higher-level discourse and activities designed to promote deep understanding within each content area (Alvermann, 2001).

Educators must also remember that learning is not an isolated activity. If teachers want their students to develop literacy skills that allow them to think as practitioners within a content area, then teachers must provide students with opportunities to engage in rich conversations with their peers and knowledgeable others to help them develop a deep understanding of content material and concepts (Heller & Greenleaf, 2007). Students whose classrooms provide reading activities followed by discourse and writing activities that reinforce and promote learning are more motivated to learn and are more likely to show learning gains than students who participate in traditional teacher-directed instruction (Guthrie et.al., 2004). Thus, developing students' literacy skills requires teachers to modify instruction to emphasize student authentic engagement and de-emphasize teacher lecture.

Critical Components of Core Literacy Instruction

As LLTs work collaboratively to develop effective literacy plans designed to improve instruction and student achievement, we suggest they include the following basic elements:

- Extended time for literacy instruction
- Direct/explicit reading comprehension strategy instruction
- Direct/explicit vocabulary development instruction
- Opportunities for academic writing in response to reading and learning
- Rigorous tasks, activities, and assignments aligned with standards and benchmarks
- Access to both independent-level and grade-level content area texts and materials
- Differentiated instruction and support determined by ongoing progress monitoring

Extended Time for Literacy Instruction. One of the essential elements of effective literacy initiatives is providing students with extended time for literacy instruction. Reeves (2003) suggests that student achievement improves when schools focus on intensive literacy instruction for up to three hours a day. Biancarosa & Snow (2004) also suggest that students should be engaged in two to four hours of literacy-connected instruction across disciplines per day. It is important to note that the expectation is not that literacy instruction supplant content area instruction but instead be embedded within content area instruction.

In order to accomplish the goal of incorporating extended time for literacy instruction, LLTs must develop a plan to help teachers begin to understand the relationship between literacy skill development and improved student learning across content areas. Teachers may need support in understanding how to utilize literacy as a tool for instruction rather than as a separate content area. Nonetheless, the integration of literacy instruction within all content classrooms is critical to improving literacy outcomes as well as the mastery of content standards.

At first, the concept of devoting two to four hours of instruction to the development of literacy skills seems overwhelming and impractical. Some schools have attempted to address this issue by placing low-performing students into separate intervention classes for up to 90 minutes a day. Unfortunately, these classes are often disconnected from core instruction and tend to be staffed with teachers who are not certified in reading. Many are beginning or alternatively certified teachers who often lack sufficient knowledge of pedagogy and have been provided with minimal professional development beyond the basic components of reading. More importantly, many of these teachers do not believe they possess the necessary skills to motivate their students to improve their reading achievement (Craig, 2006). In effect, these intervention-focused literacy plans reinforce the concept of reading as a separate content to be learned and de-emphasize the need for all teachers to address literacy as part of core instruction. They isolate reading development from the application of reading skills to content learning, significantly reducing the likelihood that students will generalize what is learned in reading intervention to content area reading. Blanket placement of underperforming students into reading intervention classes that are disconnected from core instruction isolates literacy from learning and reinforces the concept that adolescent literacy instruction is a remedial issue rather than a crucial element of all effective instruction.

We promote a more balanced approach aligned with current research. The Alliance for Excellence in Education suggests that schools focus on two essential components: literacy instruction for all students in all core subjects combined with targeted intervention for students reading two or more grade levels behind (Wise, 2009). Snow & Moje (2010) urge schools to develop plans that include three components: "continued development of general language and literacy skills; incorporating literacy into content area instruction; and supporting struggling readers" (p. 67). If this is thought of in "response to intervention" terms, effective plans include action steps that allow for Tier 1 literacy instruction across all content areas for all students combined with Tier 2 and Tier 3 literacy interventions for students who have yet to develop the literacy skills to comprehend grade-level text.

We are not suggesting this is an easy task. However, we are suggesting that developing a comprehensive literacy plan that provides effective core literacy instruction across all content areas combined with literacy intervention for students who are significantly behind is worth the time and effort, as it will improve literacy outcomes, promote content learning, and benefit all students.

Direct/Explicit Reading Comprehension Strategy Instruction. Reading strategies can be defined as "deliberate, goal-directed attempts to control and modify the reader's efforts to decode text, understand words, and construct meanings of text." (Afflerbach, Pearson, & Paris, 2008, p. 368). Directly teaching reading comprehension strategies, modeling how to use the strategies effectively, and providing students opportunities to practice applying the strategies daily over an extended period of time leads to increased reading achievement (Biancarosa & Snow, 2004; Pressley, 2001). A solid literacy plan includes pre-reading, during-reading, and post-reading comprehension instruction. Students are more apt to develop comprehension skills when they are provided with instruction and time to apply reading comprehension strategies to relevant instructional materials as part of content instruction rather than as isolated strategy instruction (Heller & Greenleaf, 2007).

One role of the LLT is to identify specific strategies to be implemented by all teachers in order to reinforce the use of the strategies with different types of texts across content areas. Identifying specific strategies to address pre, during, and post reading is an easy way to introduce comprehension instruction into the curriculum without teachers feeling they are diverting attention away from the curriculum (see Figure 5.1 on the next page). This approach encourages active reading within all classes and ensures that students make the connection between reading comprehension strategies and learning.

Pre-reading strategies, such as identifying text features to make predictions about the text, are helpful to students. Teachers begin by modeling think-alouds as an effective instructional practice that allows teachers to embed literacy instruction within content instruction. Prior to asking students to read assigned text, teachers review the relevant text features and ask students to make predictions about the topic and concepts contained in the

FIGURE 5.1 Pre-, During-, and Post-Reading Strategies

Pre-Reading Strategies	During-Reading Strategies	Post-Reading Strategies
• Previewing text • Activating prior knowledge • Making predictions	• Selectively underlining/ highlighting • Recognizing word parts • Paraphrasing • Making margin notes • Asking questions	• Taking Cornell notes • Organizing column notes • Utilizing concept maps • Using Venn diagrams • Writing summary statements • Creating graphic organizers

text. Ideally, the teacher places the assigned reading on a projection device (e.g., overhead projector, ELMO) and shows students the specific text features that help guide and prepare the reader prior to reading the actual text. The teacher may also model thinking aloud to share with students how he or she uses the text features to make predictions and identify relevant details or ideas for focus. This can be followed by allowing time for students to work in small groups to review text features and make their own predictions.

In addition to pre-reading strategies, teachers should also provide students with during-reading strategies to maintain student engagement and comprehension throughout the reading process. For example, students can be taught how to selectively highlight or underline key words and phrases as they read. If it is not possible for students to write on the text, then teachers can have students create two-column notes or write key words and phrases on sticky notes to be organized after the reading is completed. With this strategy, students are asked to identify the topic of individual paragraphs as they read and to create summary sentences for sections of text. The process of summarizing paragraphs helps keep students engaged in reading and aids comprehension, while a review of the summaries helps students grasp the important information presented in the text.

Finally, teachers need to help students engage in thinking activities after the reading is completed to allow time for students to process the notes and observations they made while they read. As discussed earlier, students can be asked to summarize the text using key concepts identified as they read. They might work in small groups to discuss the relevant details and link their details to key concepts learned through the reading. They might also work in groups to identify essential questions discovered as they read. These questions can then be used to guide further discussions about the material. Content-specific graphic organizers and note-taking strategies are also effective tools for students to organize the information and draw conclusions about the text.

In order to teach reading comprehension strategies effectively, a teacher must shift from expert deliverer of information to facilitator and coach. Instead of the teacher reading the text and identifying the relevant details, which are then distributed to the students through lecture or notes, the teacher facilitates the students' discussion and analysis of the text. In this scenario, the teacher becomes a guide to help students filter out irrelevant details in favor of relevant details and to direct students to make predictions that are then reinforced or eliminated after further investigation. Ultimately, this approach allows the teacher to shift from the imparter of all knowledge to the facilitator of authentic learning experiences. The result is that students not only learn the material, but also learn how to learn the material, thus increasing their ability to read independently with comprehension.

Direct/Explicit Vocabulary Development Instruction: Effective vocabulary instruction is necessary as a means of providing students with the background knowledge they need to comprehend text. Pre-teaching academic vocabulary not only supports students' understanding of the text and the material but also reinforces their ability to read more complex academic texts across the disciplines. Vocabulary instruction should not, however, become the focal point of instruction nor should it be taught in isolation. Instead, effective vocabulary instruction is embedded in daily lessons through short, interactive vocabulary activities.

The first step in providing effective vocabulary instruction is to carefully select essential vocabulary for students to develop a deep conceptual understanding of the content. This may include content-specific vocabulary words as well as common, nonspecialized academic vocabulary and multiple-meaning words that appear across content areas (National Institute for Literacy, 2007). For instance, mathematics teachers might focus on vocabulary that is specific to mathematics (e.g., *polygon, rhombus*) while also teaching non-specialized terms (e.g., *equation, evaluate, solve*) and content-specific interpretation of words with multiple meanings (e.g., *acute, central*) found in word problems and mathematics texts.

Teachers should also consider targeting content-specific roots, prefixes, and suffixes as an important focus for vocabulary instruction. Helping students identify prefixes, suffixes, and roots that routinely appear within the discipline helps build students' background knowledge and develops their word-attack skills, improving their ability to ascertain the meaning of unknown words when they encounter them. For instance, science teachers might want to reinforce suffixes such as *ology*, while social studies teachers might want to focus on *ism*.

After selecting the words, teachers provide students with direct, explicit instruction in conjunction with multiple exposures to the vocabulary words in context (Marzano, 2004; National Institute for Literacy, 2007). Teachers should employ a Gradual Release of Responsibility model, which allows for the direct, explicit explanation of the word and its meaning, followed by modeling of how to use the word appropriately and structured opportunities for students to utilize the vocabulary in authentic reading and writing activities with feedback. Students benefit from multiple opportunities to interact with the words in meaningful ways. In addition to these strategies, Marzano (2004) also suggests that teachers provide a visual representation of each vocabulary word as a way for students to internalize the word and its meaning. Providing students with structured activities (e.g., word sorts, cloze activities), multiple exposures, and visual supports as part of daily instruction strengthens students' knowledge and understanding of important and relevant vocabulary.

With this information in mind, LLTs should develop a core literacy plan that includes identifying research-based vocabulary acquisition strategies that can be adopted by all content areas and used across the whole school. For example, the LLT may choose to select specific prefixes and suffixes as a focus for all disciplines and then allow the different disciplines to develop vocabulary activities to help students understand how those prefixes and suffixes are relevant to the content. Including specific goals for improving vocabulary instruction across the disciplines is typically a vital element of effective literacy action plans.

Opportunities for Academic Writing in Response to Reading and Learning.
Engaging students in regular academic writing activities reinforces academic thinking as well as academic writing. Writing is a learning tool that, when implemented effectively, provides students opportunities to organize and clarify their thoughts on essential topics, which leads to deeper understanding (Vacca & Vacca, 2008). Writing requires students to construct meaning and provides insight into student thinking while enhancing students' ability "to think, make connections, and achieve clarity, logic, and precision" (Schmoker, 2011, p. 86). As teachers review students' writing, they are able to determine where meaning is breaking down and provide additional support (Bromley, 2003). Teachers who regularly incorporate writing activities into instruction

are likely to see improvements in students' abilities to express their academic thinking utilizing academic language and concepts.

Some content teachers are reluctant to incorporate writing into their curriculum because they are concerned they will be overwhelmed with grading writing mechanics. However, when teachers begin to understand that the purpose of cross-content writing activities is to assess student learning of key concepts and not to teach writing mechanics, they are able to shift their focus away from traditional grammar issues and begin to assess student learning contained in the writing.

Academic writing can take on many forms. Some teachers require students to keep journals in which students record their responses to essential questions or specific class activities. Rather than grade each student's writing each day, teachers collect journals every two or three weeks and assess selected passages chosen by the teacher or the student. Some teachers have students write responses to essential questions on note cards and collect them as exit slips, which can then be used to identify areas that need to be retaught or reviewed. Many teachers require students to explain their answers on unit exams as a means of determining what students actually know about the unit. Whatever the format, incorporating writing in response to reading and learning is a vital element of any literacy plan.

Rigorous Tasks, Activities, and Assignments Aligned With Standards and Benchmarks. Far too often, we observe students engaged in basic rather than rigorous tasks that meet the expected levels of standards and benchmarks. We recommend schools reference Webb's Depth of Knowledge levels (Webb, 2002, see Figure 5.2), to determine the complexity levels of benchmarks and the corresponding required instructional rigor. A description of instructional tasks that correspond to each DOK level is included as a means of highlighting the complexity levels of typically occurring/assigned tasks. These descriptions may serve as a starting point for teams to assess the complexity level of the tasks and assignments provided for their own students.

- ◆ **Level One:** Students are engaged in activities that require simple recall of information. Students are asked to define, memorize, recall, match, etc. Most work sheets require students to work at Level One. Examples might be observing students complete a Venn diagram or a word map. Most times, students are just copying or matching information, which requires a very low level of thinking. Having students read aloud is another example of a Level One task.
- ◆ **Level Two:** Students are engaged in developing skills and conceptual knowledge. Students might be observed working in groups to

FIGURE 5.2 Webb's Depth of Knowledge Level Descriptions

DOK Level 1	Emphasis is on facts and simple recall of previously taught information. This also means following simple steps, recipes, or directions, which can be difficult without requiring reasoning. Students find "the right answer," and there is no debating the "correctness"; it is either right or wrong.
DOK Level 2	Students compare two or more concepts, finding similarities and differences, and applying factual learning at the basic skill level. Students identify the main ideas, which requires deeper knowledge than just the definition. Students must explain "how" or "why" and often estimate or interpret to respond.
DOK Level 3	Students must reason or plan to find an acceptable solution to a problem. More than one correct response or approach is possible. This requires complex or abstract thinking and the application of knowledge or skill in a new and unique situation.
DOK Level 4	Students typically identify a problem, plan a course of action, enact that plan, and make decisions based on collected data. More time than one class period is usually necessary. Multiple solutions are possible, and students often connect multiple content areas to come up with unique and creative solutions.

Webb, 2002

make inferences, categorize information, identify patterns, construct knowledge, or summarize information. Students might be working with graphic organizers *and* explaining their knowledge verbally or in writing. Care must be taken to make sure that graphic organizers are not simply being used as a Level One tool, with which students are expected to copy information into the graphic as opposed to using the organizer to develop understanding. In this regard, having students explain their conclusions through short, written responses is critical to developing Level Two tasks. In this case, students might be observed categorizing a list of words and then explaining in a short response why they chose those categories and why each word fits the category.

◆ **Level Three:** Students are now engaged in strategic-thinking activities and complicated tasks that require them to construct new meaning, formulate hypotheses based on new information, and develop logical arguments. At this level, students are taking ownership of the learning process. Students might be observed collecting information, formulating a hypothesis, and then presenting their ideas to the class through oral or written responses. They are able to support their ideas with clearly identified details and information. An example might include students determining an author's purpose after identifying essential elements of the text (i.e., text structures, word choice, visual examples), determining their relevance to the main idea, making inferences as to why the author chose these specific elements, and drawing conclusions about the author's purpose.

◆ **Level Four:** Students are now engaged in the highest level of Webb's DOK. They are synthesizing information to develop new hypotheses. Students might be observed collecting information from a specific time period, genre, or author to develop a fully defined hypothesis that is supported with specific details. Students working at this level are required to collect and analyze information, make predictions, develop a logical argument to support their hypothesis, and apply what they have learned to novel, read-world situations or problems.

Note that each level builds on the previous level. In order for students to categorize, they must first identify. In order for students to engage in strategic thinking, they must first identify relevant details, categorize the details, and develop a hypothesis as to the conclusions that can be drawn from the details. As teachers work collaboratively to unpack the benchmarks, they develop their understanding not only of what the test measures but also of which instructional tasks and activities are necessary to prepare students to master the standards.

Access to Both Grade-Level and Independent-Level Text. Schools must work to significantly intensify literacy instruction within core content areas and to encourage students to read in all classes throughout the school day. An intervention-focused plan in the absence of strong core instruction and student engagement in reading across content areas will not result in remediation of students who are significantly behind in reading.

Unfortunately, "the current situation in many schools is that struggling readers participate in 30 to 60 minutes of appropriate reading intervention instruction and then spend the remaining five hours a day sitting in class-rooms with texts they cannot read, cannot learn to read from, cannot learn sci-ence or social studies from" (Allington, 2009, p. 29). Instead of this approach, Allington recommends that schools provide students with content area text and reading assignments that are written at students' individual reading levels in addition to grade-level text. Not surprisingly, struggling readers are much more likely to engage in reading and acquire critical content knowledge when provided with texts and materials that are written at their independent reading level than when provided only with grade-level text (Mathes et al., 2005). Providing students with access to Lexile-leveled classroom librar-ies and technology resources that can transform grade-level text into more-readable independent-level text is a good first step to providing true access to content material and frequent opportunities to practice reading.

Differentiated Instruction and Formative Assessment. We have found that many teachers cringe when the words *differentiated instruction* are mentioned. This reaction is related to the misassumption that providing differentiated instruc-tion requires teachers to design individual lesson plans for every student in their classroom. The reality is that most teachers informally engage in differ-entiated instruction as part of regular instruction. When teachers stop to help a student who is struggling with a task, they are differentiating instruction. When calling a group of students together to talk about something confusing to them, teachers are differentiating instruction. What we are asking teachers to do now is to formalize the process so they can target identified students, utilize appropriate data to understand student needs, and provide appropri-ate scaffolding strategies to help students when they are presented with new information and/or skills. Over time, these scaffolds are removed slowly as students become more adept, a process that is also informed by data.

Regularly incorporating formative assessments into and throughout instruction helps guide the planning and delivery of differentiated instruc-tion. Formative assessments are "all those activities undertaken by teachers, and/or by their students, that provide information to be used as feedback to modify the teaching and learning activities in which they are engaged" (Black & Wiliam, 1998, p. 8). Unlike summative assessment, which is typi-cally completed at the end of a learning cycle and measures what students have learned as a result *of* instruction, formative assessment is administered before, during, and at the end of instruction and provides information *for* instructional planning (Pellegrino, Chudowsky, & Glaser, 2001). Whether or not an assessment is formative in nature is determined not by the assess-ment itself but by how the assessment data is used. For instance, typically summative assessment data (e.g., state assessments, final exams) can become formative if the data from the assessments is used to make instructional decisions, such as which students need reteaching or which parts of the curriculum require additional time and focus. Thus, assessments become formative in nature only when teachers use the information to adapt instruction to meet student needs and advance them toward learning goals (Shavelson, Black, William, & Coffey, 2003).

Formative assessments help answer three central questions that are critical to planning effective differentiation:

1. What has the student learned in relation to the learning goal?
2. Is there a difference between what the student has learned and what he or she was expected to learn as a result of instruction?
3. Why is there a difference between what the student has learned and what he or she was expected to learn?

By setting clear learning goals and then assessing student learning against the learning goals, teachers can determine gaps between what learning is expected and what learning actually occurs. If the assessment data indicates that many or most students did not meet the learning goal, teachers should provide additional instruction for all students. If the assessment data indicates that only a few students did not meet learning goals, additional small-group instruction should be provided for only those students who require it to meet the learning goals. Efforts should be made to determine *why* students did not learn what was expected, as this information should be used to plan additional instruction. Often, this information can be gleaned from analyzing existing assessment data but sometimes may require additional assessment.

Multitiered Literacy Supports Example

The following multitiered system of support is an example of one school's plan.

Tier 1 Instruction—Cross Content Reading Instruction

School-wide foci determined after an analysis of state reading assessment outcome data revealed less than 80% of students reading at or above grade level.

Cross content reading instruction includes the following:

- ◆ Daily explicit vocabulary instruction in all courses
- ◆ Daily in-class reading of grade-level text supported by the application of of pre-, during-, and after-reading comprehension strategies
- ◆ Monthly, nonfiction reading beyond course texts in all content courses
- ◆ Academic writing in response to reading at least monthly in all courses
- ◆ Leveled texts and materials in core academic courses to allow students to practice reading and access content information

Tier 2 Intervention—Supplemental Reading Instruction

Students whose reading skills are below grade level but less than two years below grade level are placed in reading intervention courses with highly qualified instructors. The purpose of these courses is to meet the proximal literacy needs of students in order to increase students' access to grade-level texts and materials, address reading skill gaps, and prevent course failures.

Supplemental reading instruction includes the following:

- ◆ Daily explicit, modeled, guided, and independent instruction in reading intervention strategies utilizing both independent-level and grade-level text
- ◆ Daily vocabulary instruction targeting vocabulary relevant to grade-level courses
- ◆ Daily word study and word analysis instruction
- ◆ Daily, supported reading of grade-level text including independent reading with conferencing and partner reading
- ◆ Weekly academic writing activities in response to reading
- ◆ Flexible grouping to address skill gaps related to fluency and decoding skills
- ◆ Goal setting and monthly progress monitoring of students' progress on comprehending grade-level text

Tier 3 Intervention—Targeted, Individualized Reading Intervention

Students whose reading skills are two or more years below grade level or who are not responding sufficiently to Tier 2 intervention supports are placed in a 90-minute reading intervention course with highly qualified instructors.

The purpose of these courses is to meet the proximal literacy needs of students in order to increase students' access to grade-level texts and prevent course failures while closing significant skill gaps over time.

Targeted reading instruction includes the following:

- Daily explicit, modeled, guided, and independent instruction in reading intervention strategies utilizing both independent-level and grade-level text
- Daily vocabulary instruction targeting vocabulary relevant to grade-level courses
- Daily word study and word analysis instruction
- Daily, supported reading of grade-level text including independent reading with conferencing and partner reading
- Weekly academic writing activities in response to reading
- Flexible grouping to address skill gaps related to fluency and decoding

AND

- Individualized intensive instruction to address significant word attack and reading fluency skill gaps
- Goal setting and weekly progress monitoring of skill development and general outcome improvements
- Bi-weekly data chats between student and teacher to review progress, celebrate when appropriate, and make necessary changes to instructional program

Conclusion

While we recognize the complexity of developing a core literacy plan that includes all the critical components necessary to maximize student literacy outcomes, we believe that the time and energy required to build and implement an effective plan are worth the effort. Implementing an effective core literacy plan has the best chance of meeting the needs of all students. When most students' needs are met through core instruction, the school will be able to accurately identify students who may need supplemental instruction to master grade-level literacy standards. Meeting these students' needs is best accomplished through the implementation of tiered intervention supports that are aligned with core instruction. Having a clearly defined core literacy program is critical to the development of tiered interventions that function to support students' mastery of core literacy goals.

6

Tiered Literacy Intervention

... test scores will take care of themselves if educators commit to ensuring that each student masters essential skills and concepts in every unit of instruction, align their practices and resources toward that purpose, and discontinue many traditional practices that do not serve that purpose.
—DuFour, DuFour, Eaker, & Karhanek, 2004, p. 27

An emphasis on early reading intervention (i.e., kindergarten through third grade) has resulted in significant improvements in elementary reading outcomes, with the percentage of elementary students meeting proficiency standards increasing steadily within recent decades (UNESCO Institute for Statistics, 2008). Unfortunately, effective early literacy programming and high rates of proficient elementary students do not guarantee that these same students will continue to be proficient readers as they pass through the middle grades and onto high school. As the demands of reading grade-level text increase substantially, both in terms of length and complexity, and literacy instruction wanes, once-proficient students may begin to experience difficulty meeting increasing literacy demands. To make matters worse, a significant proportion of students arrive in secondary schools without ever mastering basic reading skills or demonstrating reading proficiency at any grade level. As a result, secondary schools face the difficult challenge of remediating skill gaps while providing enough literacy support to allow students to master grade-level content material.

This challenge has proven a difficult one. Despite the consistent reading gains among students in kindergarten through third grade and with fourth-grade students scoring among the best in the world, many students either drop out of high school or graduate without the literacy skills necessary to be successful in college or competitive in the workforce. In fact, U.S. tenth graders score among the lowest in the world (UNESCO Institute for Statistics, 2008), and this trend has existed with virtually no improvement for almost two decades. While some of these students will adequately respond to core literacy instruction and differentiation, many others will require additional instruction to meet grade-level expectations.

Although a significant percentage of students enter middle and high schools every year with literacy skills that are insufficient to allow them to comprehend grade-level text, most secondary schools take a "wait and see" approach to the problem. Instead of immediately providing students with intervention to address their skill deficits and literacy needs within content area classes, schools often wait to see if students will be successful in their courses without additional support. Unfortunately, students who cannot comprehend the grade-level texts are significantly more likely to fail their courses, fall behind in credits, fail to achieve the GPA required for graduation, and ultimately become off track for on-time high school graduation. The more off track a student becomes (e.g., further behind in credits, lower GPA), the more likely the student is to drop out of school altogether. In fact, every ninth-grade course a student fails places him or her at significant risk for dropout. A review of the dropout prevention literature reveals that only 70% of students who earn one F within a semester during ninth grade and only 55% of students earning two Fs over the course of two semesters in ninth grade are likely to graduate on time, while students with three or more Fs are very unlikely to graduate from high school without significant intervention (Heppen & Bowles Therriault, 2008).

The link between reading below grade level and course failure is not surprising when one considers the fact that reading serves as a major foundational skill for all school-based learning (Lesnick, George, Smithgall, Gwynne, 2010). Students with below grade-level reading skills often have difficulty keeping pace with their proficient peers, a problem that is exacerbated by the increasing educational demands at each grade level. As a result, below-level readers become further and further off track for graduation, which significantly increases the likelihood they will drop out (Hernandez, 2011). In fact, approximately 23% of students with significant reading deficits fail to graduate from high school on time compared to only 4% of proficient readers. The impact of reading deficits on the graduation rates of students from low socioeconomic (SES) backgrounds is even more devastating, with 26% of low SES, nonproficient readers leaving high school without a diploma, representing a rate of nearly six times the dropout rate of low-SES, proficient readers (Hernandez, 2011).

As adults, nonproficient readers are less likely than proficient readers to be employed and more likely to earn incomes below the poverty level (Kutner et al., 2007) and be incarcerated (Harlow, 2003). The impact of literacy problems is far-reaching and significant for individual students and for

FIGURE 6.1 School A—High-Performing School Five-Year Trend Data

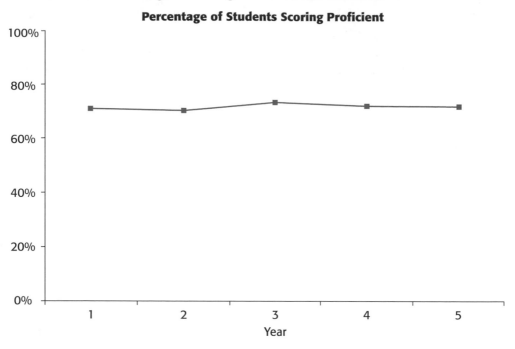

society as a whole. Consequently, secondary schools really have no choice but to provide the support and interventions required to close literacy skill gaps and to prevent course failures.

Anticipating the Literacy Needs of Students

No one who works in a school should be surprised that every year some students require intervention to meet grade-level standards. Schools not only can accurately predict that they will have students in need of tiered intervention supports but can also very closely estimate the percentage and number of nonproficient students who will need to be served. This information is critical for the planning of master schedules and the allocation of resources (e.g., time, personnel, and space) to support tiered intervention supports and should be analyzed and understood prior to making such important decisions.

Reviewing Literacy Trend Data. Teams can accurately predict the percentage and number of students who will likely require intervention to meet grade-level standards by reviewing their school's literacy trend data. In our experience, school trend data is typically flat, given the absence of a significant

FIGURE 6.2 School B–Low-Performing School Five-Year Trend Data

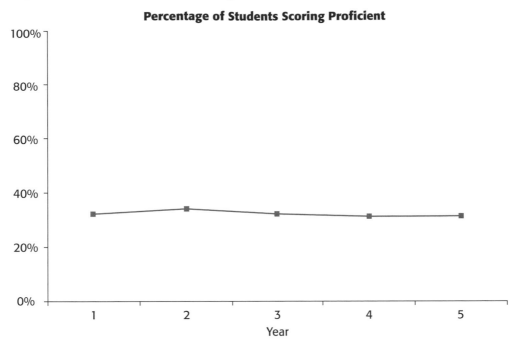

Percentage of Students Scoring Proficient

organizational change, and thus can be utilized to accurately predict the school's intervention needs. Graphically representing the percentage of students who score proficient on the state's standardized reading assessment helps paint this picture. Consider the two examples provided. Figure 6.1 represents the trend data of School A, a typically regarded high-performing high school, while Figure 6.2 represents the trend data of School B, considered one of the same district's lowest-performing schools.

Notice that although the high-performing high school (School A) had a greater percentage of students scoring within the proficient range compared to the low-performing high school (School B), both schools' trend lines are virtually flat, indicating very little change in the percentage of students in need of intervention every year. Without major organizational changes, School A could anticipate that every year approximately 28% of its students would need some kind of literacy support to master grade-level standards, while School B would face an overwhelming 68% of students in need of literacy support. This information was critical for both school and district strategic planning. At the school level, leadership teams were faced with the challenge of providing literacy supports that matched their students' needs both in intensity and in focus. This feat, although difficult at School A, with 28% of its student body needing support, was quite nearly impossible at School B without significant restructuring of the school day and substantial support and resource allocation from the district. In this case, with the support of the district leadership, School B extended its school day by one hour for all students. The additional hour allowed for intervention for identified students who required additional literacy instruction and extension and enrichment for students who did not. Consequently, all nonproficient students received between one and three periods of reading intervention every day, depending on the intensity of their needs. This change represented an enormous commitment to the students at School B on the part of the school's faculty, who agreed to teach an additional hour every day; the district, which allocated funds to increase the salaries of the school's staff; and students and parents, who were required to rearrange schedules to account for more time spent at school. Although everyone involved made sacrifices to provide the school's students with increased literacy support, it is a common sentiment that the change allowed the school to accomplish a previously unattainable feat (providing nearly 70% of its student body with reading intervention) that was not only warranted but quite frankly paramount to improving the school's academic outcomes.

Designing Effective Intervention Programs

The design of effective literacy intervention programs requires that secondary school personnel possess a thorough understanding of their current and incoming students' literacy data. This understanding is critical to establishing the "compelling why" of intervention efforts and informing the design of literacy intervention programming that is matched to the needs of incoming and current students. Ideally, secondary schools should know the literacy needs of their incoming students six to nine months prior to their transition. This time frame would greatly facilitate the school's ability to design a master schedule that allows for the implementation of a multitiered system of student supports. Of course, access to literacy data is not enough; school teams must also systematically analyze and interpret the data. Secondary schools that do not have access to literacy data, particularly student diagnostic data, and/or do not have school personnel with skills to thoroughly analyze the data will find the process of building an effective literacy intervention program difficult if not impossible.

Utilizing Student Data to Drive Intervention Decisions

Universal Screening. As mentioned in earlier chapters, identifying students in need of literacy intervention rarely requires the collection of additional screening data, as each secondary student typically comes with years of data that paints a clear picture of his or her risk level. Thus, unlike at the elementary level, where universal screening consists of the administration of one or more reading assessments to all students, at the secondary level, universal screening is accomplished by reviewing students' literacy assessment data from prior school years. Reviewing existing state assessment or other universally available literacy data prior to the beginning of the school year allows for the identification of students in need of intervention and the development of an effective master schedule that includes appropriate multitiered supports.

Diagnostic Data. While a review of existing data is vital to determining which students need literacy intervention, it typically offers little information regarding *what* students need to close skill gaps and master grade-level reading material. While some state reading assessments provide information regarding a student's proficiency within general reading categories, few if any provide specific enough information to plan ongoing supplemental or targeted intervention. For instance, Florida's state assessment provides information regarding student performance in four general categories (Cluster 1: words and phrases in contexts; Cluster 2: main idea, plot, and purpose; Cluster 3: comparisons, cause and effect; and Cluster 4: reference and research) (Florida Department of Education, 2010) but lends no information about *why* a group of students or a particular student performed poorly in one or more cluster area. Thus, understanding *why* students are struggling typically requires the collection and analysis of diagnostic reading data.

The Purpose of Tiered Intervention Supports

The purpose of tiered intervention supports is to ensure that students successfully achieve grade-level standards and expectations. Thus, tiered intervention supports must be aligned and integrated with core instruction. In order for this to be accomplished, intervention providers must be fluent in the standards and goals that drive core instruction and be kept abreast of the skill and/or engagement barriers that preclude their students from achieving the expected achievement levels.

As illustrated in Figure 6.3 (page 98), Tier 2 and Tier 3 interventions do not supplant Tier 1 core instruction. Instead, tiered intervention supports should rest firmly on effective core instruction and be designed to allow for additional explicit instruction, practice, and review beyond what is available in core instruction. In the absence of core instruction, tiered interventions are

FIGURE 6.3 Aligned and Integrated Intervention Programs

Reproduced with permission from the Florida PS/RTI Project

likely to seem disconnected and disjointed to students and are unlikely to improve student outcomes in their core courses.

Tier 2 Intervention. Tier 2 interventions should be provided as a supplement to core instruction as a means of addressing student reading skill deficits and providing additional time for practice and review. Tier 2 interventions are ideally provided within small-group settings (six to ten students) in order to maximize each student's opportunity to have his or her needs addressed. Groups should be formed based on common underlying literacy needs to allow for targeted intervention. It should not be assumed that nonproficient students with the same reading level share the same underlying reasons for their reading difficulties. Instead, teams should collect and analyze diagnostic data to determine underlying skill deficits and form groups according to common needs.

Let's consider a case example by examining the student data presented in Figure 6.4 (page 99). Within this example, two students whose general outcome data, in this case the probability of scoring proficient on a state standardized reading assessment, indicate very similar reading levels. However, each student's diagnostic data indicates that there are differing reasons for Student 1's and Student 2's reading issues. While Student 1's data indicates that reading fluency issues may be precluding her from comprehending grade-level text, Student 2's data indicates he possesses sufficient word analysis and reading

FIGURE 6.4 Student 1 and Student 2 General Outcome and Diagnostic Data

	Probability of Success	Comprehension Percentile Rank	Fluency Percentile Rank	Word Analysis Percentile Rank
Student 1	37%	40th Percentile	19th Percentile	60th Percentile
Student 2	39%	38th Percentile	61st Percentile	58th Percentile

Note: These data represent student data collected from a state online progress-monitoring assessment.

Probability of Success: The data indicate the probability of student success on a state reading assessment. It is determined by comparing the student's current comprehension level with past performance on the state exam.

Comprehension Percentile Rank: Students are provided up to three passages to read. Passages are selected based on student performance on previous passages and are dependent upon student performance on the previous passage. For example, if a student scores poorly on the previous passage, the next passage is at a lower Lexile level. Comprehension is thus reported based on students' independent reading level.

Fluency Percentile Rank: Student fluency is measured through a MAZE test. Students are provided with two grade-level passages to read. They choose the appropriate words from a drop-down menu. They are allowed two minutes on each passage.

Word Analysis Percentile Rank: Students listen to words and then are asked to spell the words. Teachers can access the students' spelling to determine which words students misspell and identify patterns that indicate student word analysis concerns.

fluency skills to comprehend text. Instead of focusing on improving his fluency or word attack skills, is likely Student 2 would benefit from additional explicit instruction in reading comprehension strategies and/or vocabulary development. It would be a mistake to place these two students in the same Tier 2 intervention group because their intervention needs are different. Placed in a group focused on fluency, Student 2 would likely become disengaged. He may in fact become a more fluent reader, but he will continue to lack the reading comprehension skills and/or vocabulary to comprehend grade-level text. Similarly, if Student 1 is placed in an intervention group that does not include strategies to improve reading fluency, she is unlikely to read more fluently, and her reading comprehension will consequently not improve. Both students have intact word analysis/decoding skills. Therefore, placing either of the students into an intervention group that focuses on decoding and word analysis will likely not be effective in improving their reading comprehension skills.

Although addressing students' skill deficits is critical to improving their ability to comprehend grade-level text, these skills should not be taught in isolation, but rather integrated into larger units of instruction that focus on the application of the skill to allow for comprehension of text (Langer, 2001). Therefore, in addition to explicit instruction to address students' skill deficits, intervention teachers must provide opportunities for their students to practice the skills within the context of authentic reading tasks.

In addition to explicitly addressing student basic skill deficits (e.g., decoding, fluency), intervention teachers should provide direct instruction in comprehension strategies with increasingly complex text. Comprehension strategy instruction provides students with a cognitive framework for monitoring their understanding and making repairs when comprehension breaks down. Student comprehension significantly improves when they are taught metacognitive strategies to employ before, during, and after reading, such as activating prior knowledge, predicting, asking questions, summarizing, and organizing and assimilating new information into what they already know (Langer, 2001). In order for comprehension strategies to be mastered and generalized to reading outside the reading intervention classroom, strategy instruction must include explicit instruction in how, when, and why to apply specific strategies and provide students with numerous opportunities to apply the comprehension strategies across multiple and varying texts (Pressley, 2000). As with basic skill instruction, comprehension strategy instruction should not be taught in isolation, but rather should include explicit, modeled, and guided instruction utilizing the students' content area or other grade-level text (Pressley, 2000). Students' application of comprehension strategies should be monitored along with their progress in reading comprehension. Feedback related to students' effective use of comprehension strategies should be provided along with information regarding their reading comprehension progress. Both pieces of information should be shared with students and their parents on a regular basis (Langer, 2001).

Because many below-level readers have significant vocabulary deficits, it is often necessary for intervention teachers to provide explicit vocabulary instruction as part of their intervention program. Vocabulary instruction should begin with explicit instruction in word meanings and a discussion about contexts to which the word could be applied. As with comprehension strategy instruction, students should be provided with multiple opportunities to apply the words within a variety of contexts; it is also important for students to encounter the vocabulary words within text (Marzano, Pickering & Pollock, 2001). Providing students with opportunities to actively process and apply the vocabulary words, such as asking students to respond to reading comprehension questions utilizing the vocabulary words taught as part of the current or prior lessons, further solidifies students' acquisition of the vocabulary words (Curtis & Longo, 2001).

Tier 2 intervention should not be regarded as time devoted to test preparation or provided in lieu of or isolated from instruction designed to support students' mastery of grade-level standards. Instead, intervention teachers should work to integrate test preparation into instruction, providing multiple opportunities over time to develop test-taking competencies as they relate to the curriculum (Langer, 2001).

Tier 3 Intervention. Effective Tier 3 literacy interventions typically possess all the characteristics represented in high-quality Tier 2 intervention programs, including explicit instruction to address basic skill deficits, direct comprehension strategy and vocabulary instruction, and integrated test preparation. While intervention focus does not characteristically differ substantially between Tier 2 and Tier 3 intervention programs, significant differences are typical regarding the amount of intervention time and intervention personalization provided to students. As such, Tier 3 interventions are typically provided to students within smaller intervention groups than are typical for Tier 2 interventions (two to five students versus six to ten).

Intervention teachers should design Tier 3 interventions to meet the specific needs of individual students. This personalization of intervention is made possible through the administration and interpretation of individual diagnostic assessments that reveal each student's individual learning needs (Batsche et al., 2006).

Unlike within elementary RTI models, students with significantly below-level reading skills should not be required to respond to Tier 2 intervention before receiving the most intense interventions (Tier 3) (Fuchs, Fuchs, & Compton, 2010). Instead, teams should calculate the difference between a student's current reading level (e.g., fourth-grade reading level) and his or her expected reading level (e.g., ninth grade) and compare the number of years behind to the number of years available to bring the student up to grade level in order to determine the most appropriate intervention intensity.

For instance, a student who enters ninth grade with a fourth-grade reading level has, in the best-case scenario, four years to make nine years' worth of growth, if the goal is for the student to graduate from high school with reading skills similar to his or her proficient peers. The reality is, students who enter high school more than two years behind in reading are significantly more likely to drop out of school (Hernandez, 2011) within the first two years of high school (Bridgeland, Dilulio, & Burke Morison, 2006). As a result, high schools may not be able to count on more than two years with the most at-risk students, especially if intensive interventions are not provided immediately upon a student's entry. Given this reality, it is best practice to provide students who enter either middle or high schools significantly behind their peers with the most intense intervention opportunities available.

Utilizing Research-Based Intervention

A school's multitiered intervention program should utilize research-based interventions whenever possible, as scientifically validated interventions provide the school with the "best shot at implementing strategies that will be effective for a large majority of students" (Batsche et al., 2006, p. 20). Because there are limited proven reading intervention programs for middle and high school students, teams may be forced to select intervention programs with a limited research base or with a research base that involves students unlike their student body (e.g., white, high-SES students versus Hispanic, low-SES students). Even with the best of intentions, given the current research base for adolescent literacy programming, teams may have no choice but to select intervention strategies/programs with a limited or mismatched research base. Under these conditions, teams should consider the implementation of the intervention strategies/programs experimental in nature and plan to monitor the impact of the strategies/programs on student outcomes more closely than would be necessary with more proven strategies/programs.

We are often asked by school teams, "What reading interventions are other schools using?" This question demonstrates the assumption held by many school teams that a reading intervention program that has proven effective at one school will produce the exact same results at another school. It would be nice if intervention programming was this simple, but unfortunately it is not. School teams should not assume that any single intervention strategy or program, regardless of its research base or its effectiveness at another school, will meet the needs of every student. Instead, teams should utilize diagnostic data to match research-based intervention strategies/programs to the specific needs of their students. Thus, the *best* intervention program is the one designed to meet the specific needs of the school's below-level readers.

Evaluating the Effectiveness of Tiered Interventions

Monitoring the impact and effectiveness of tiered intervention supports is critical both in terms of ensuring that students are receiving the necessary intensity and type of intervention and to assess the cost-benefit ratio of various intervention programs. Teams should consistently consult the data to assess whether the investment of time, personnel, space, and money required for implementation of a specific intervention is getting the desired results.

Unfortunately, because many schools do not adequately evaluate the impact of their intervention programs, we have witnessed many schools implementing ineffective or even harmful intervention programs for years on end. These schools not only waste precious resources on ineffective programs but also fail to recognize the need to change their intervention programs in order to better serve their students. As a result, consensus around the belief that anything can be done to improve student outcomes at the school wanes, and students continue to struggle without much hope of support. Although common, this situation can be avoided if schools develop and implement an assessment calendar and regularly scheduled data reviews.

The more intensive the intervention supports, the more closely the impact on student literacy should be monitored. Hence, school teams should plan to collect skill specific data (e.g., fluency, decoding, comprehension strategy application) biweekly from students receiving Tier 2 intervention and weekly from students receiving Tier 3 intervention. Additionally, all students receiving intervention should be administered a reading comprehension assessment once monthly. Collecting both skill and comprehension data is essential because each allows teams to answer critical questions. Skill assessment data allows teams to answer the question, "Are the students' basic skills improving as a result of intervention?" while comprehension assessment data allows teams to assess whether improvements in basic skills are translating to sufficient improvements in reading comprehension. Finally, teams should assess the impact of intervention programs on successful course completion. In other words, at least once a quarter teams should consult the data to examine whether students receiving literacy intervention are at least as likely to pass their courses, remain in school, and graduate on time as their already-proficient peers. Schools should change intervention programs that result in less-than-desirable outcomes.

Characteristics of Effective Intervention Programs

The literacy issues of below-level readers have the potential to negatively impact student learning across all content areas. No single content area (e.g., mathematics, science, social studies, art) is immune to the impact of students' inability to glean relevant information from grade-level text. Consequently, the responsibility to provide needed literacy intervention and support should not be placed solely on the shoulders of specific content areas (e.g., language arts) or individual teachers. Instead, literacy intervention should be designed as part of a school-wide system of student supports, allowing interventions to be proactive rather than reactive, as well as systematic, timely, and directive (DuFour, DuFour, Eaker, Karhanek, 2004).

From Remediation to Prevention and Intervention. It is critical for schools to shift from a remedial framework in which students are provided additional support only after they have failed to a framework that is focused on prevention, providing intervention as soon as a student begins to show signs of struggle (DuFour et al., 2004). The cost of course failures, both literally and in terms of student disengagement, is immense. In fact, ninth-grade course failures are more predictive of high school dropouts than are standardized test scores (Kennelly & Monrad, 2007). Students who enter secondary schools with below-level reading skills are at a higher risk for disengagement and course failures than are their proficient peers. Thus, time and energy devoted to supporting students' literacy needs and improving the likelihood that they will acquire the knowledge and skills to obtain credit for their courses are resources well spent. Ultimately, this approach saves schools time and energy that would otherwise need to be spent in course recovery and reengagement programs.

From Random to Systematic Response. Many secondary schools provide intervention for students through a primarily informal system within which the availability of intervention time is dependent on whether individual teachers decide to provide it. Within this system, intervention time and procedures are random because they are dependent on the responses of individuals. Consequently, some students may have access to intervention, while others, whose teachers choose not to provide intervention, do not. Instead of a random response, DuFour and his colleagues (2004) recommend an intervention system in which interventions exist within a school-wide plan that is understood and utilized by all staff. The school-wide plan allows schools to move away from random intervention to a systemic, consistently applied intervention program.

From Reactive to Proactive. As discussed earlier, developing a system of student supports that allow for the prevention of course failures through a timely response to student needs is essential (DuFour et al., 2004). Waiting to intervene until students have failed content courses places the students at significant risk for dropping out. Instead, a school should anticipate the needs of students by analyzing the school's trend data and students' historical reading data to answer two key questions: (1) What percentage of students are likely to require intervention to meet grade-level standards, and (2) In which specific literacy areas are they most likely to require support (e.g., vocabulary, fluency)? The answers to these questions should be used to guide the leadership team's development of intervention programs prior to the beginning of the school year. Having literacy interventions in place before the school year begins allows identified students to receive support from the first day of school. Further, students who were not initially identified as having literacy intervention needs but who begin to experience difficulties, as well as new students who transfer in with literacy intervention needs, can quickly gain access to the literacy supports and need not fail before being identified and served.

From Invitational to Directive. Perhaps because of the difficulty of manipulating master schedules to include intervention time and the common sentiment among secondary educators that secondary students should take responsibility for their own learning, virtually all the secondary schools in which we have worked have provided intervention opportunities for students solely before and after school and sometimes during the students' lunch period. These opportunities are sometimes informal, often requiring students to request tutoring from a teacher. Other times, the school has organized a more formal "extended learning program" with specific teachers and subjects available to provide tutoring on specific days. It is left up to the student to come before or stay after school to take advantage of the academic support.

We have come to expect these types of invitational intervention programs. We have also come to expect, and have yet to be proven wrong, that the students most in need of academic support and intervention rarely attend the invitational intervention programs. We are not the only ones who are aware of this problem. We often ask educators, "Who is not likely to attend invitational intervention programs, particularly those that occur before or after school?" Without fail, the educators respond, "Those who most need the intervention." Plain and simple, invitational intervention programs do not work in most cases, especially for the most at-risk students. Whether or not students *should* choose to attend invitational intervention programs is neither here nor there. The fact is that they do not attend and consequently do not receive the intervention they need to be successful in school.

A good friend and colleague of ours once told her leadership team, "Teenagers are like cakes ten minutes before the kitchen timer goes off. They look fully done, but inside they are still gooey." Although adolescents often look like full-grown adults, they may lack the insight and discipline to *choose* to seek out or attend available intervention programs. Consequently, educators must build intervention time and programs into their master schedules so they can direct students to attend and more effectively monitor their attendance. The result will be improved student outcomes (DuFour et al., 2004).

Figure 6.5: Sample Ninth-Grade Master Schedule (page 107) offers an example of one school's ninth-grade master schedule. The master schedule provides multiple opportunities for students to receive intervention within their regular school day. For example, there are reading intervention courses, both single and double block, to ensure that all students in need of reading intervention have access. These courses are typically reserved for students with significant reading issues (reading two or more years below grade level.) The school also has built-in literacy supports for math and science for students whose reading issues might prevent them from being successful in these content courses. These courses are typically scheduled for students whose reading abilities are approaching grade level but who are likely to struggle with reading the grade-level text and/or providing written responses.

In addition to these intervention courses, the school has also included a credit-generating elective course called Critical Thinking for all ninth-grade students. This course serves as an intervention support for students who need supplemental instruction to successfully complete their courses and as enrichment for students who are not in need of intervention support. Each student is scheduled into the Critical Thinking course with a teacher whose content area expertise (e.g., reading, math, science) best matches the student's needs. Students for whom reading is the greatest need are scheduled into Critical Thinking courses taught by reading and language arts teachers. Students for whom mathematics is the greatest need are scheduled into Critical Thinking courses taught by math teachers. Students who are not in need of intervention are scheduled into Critical Thinking courses taught by physical education or fine arts teachers.

This intervention structure has resulted in a significant decline (i.e., greater than 50%) in the percentage of students who fail courses in ninth grade. As a result, the school has witnessed a great improvement in student engagement rates as well as the percentage of students remaining on track for graduation. The school also has had to invest significantly fewer resources into credit recovery options over time and has redirected these resources to further support successful ninth-grade transition.

FIGURE 6.5 Sample Ninth-Grade Master Schedule

Teacher	Dept	1st	2nd	3rd	4th	5th	6th	7th
Teacher 1	Language Arts	Eng I Hon	Eng I	Eng I	Critical Thinking	Eng I Hon	Eng I	Planning
Teacher 2	Language Arts	Eng I Hon	Eng I	Eng I	Critical Thinking	Eng I	Eng I Hon	Planning
Teacher 3	Exceptional Student Education; Language Arts		Eng I	Eng I	Critical Thinking	Eng I	Eng I	Planning
Teacher 4	Exceptional Student Education; Math	Algebra I	Algebra I	Algebra I	Critical Thinking	Algebra I	Algebra I	Planning
Teacher 5	Math	Algebra I	Algebra I	Algebra I	Critical Thinking	Algebra I	Algebra I	Planning
Teacher 6	Math	Algebra I	Geometry Hon	Geometry Hon	Critical Thinking	Algebra I	Algebra I	Planning
Teacher 7	PE	HOPE	Planning	Physical Education	Critical Thinking	HOPE	HOPE	HOPE
Teacher 8	PE	Beg/Int Weight Training	Int/Adv Weight Training	Beg/Int Weight Training	DUTY	HOPE	HOPE	Planning
Teacher 9	Math Intervention	Intensive Math: Geometry	Intensive Math: Algebra	Intensive Math: Algebra	Critical Thinking	Intensive Math: Algebra	Intensive Math: Algebra	Planning

FIGURE 6.5 Sample Ninth-Grade Master Schedule (*continued*)

Teacher	Dept	1st	2nd	3rd	4th	5th	6th	7th
Teacher 10	Reading Intervention	Literacy Support for Math	Literacy Support for Science	Intensive Reading **Single Period**	Critical Thinking	Reading Intervention **Double Block**	Reading Intervention **Double Block**	Planning
Teacher 11	Reading Intervention	Intensive Reading	Intensive Reading	Intensive Reading	Critical Thinking	Intensive Reading	Intensive Reading	Planning
Teacher 12	Science	Biology	Biology	Biology	Critical Thinking	Biology	Biology Hon	Planning
Teacher 13	Science	Biology Honors	Biology Honors	Biology Honors	Physics	Critical Thinking	Biology	Planning
Teacher 14	Science	Biology	Physical Science	Physical Science	Critical Thinking	Biology	Biology	Planning
Teacher 15	Social Studies	Psychology I/II	Law Studies/LS Concepts	Comp Law	Planning	Critical Thinking	Psychology I/II	Law Studies/LS Concepts
Teacher 16	Fine Arts	Art 2D Comp I	Art 3D 1	Planning	Critical Thinking	Art 3D Comp I	Art 2D Comp 1	Art 2D Comp 1
Teacher 17	Career and Tech.	Intro to Information Technology (9th grade)			Critical Thinking	Planning		Intro to Information Technology (9th grade)
Teacher 18	Fine Arts	Drama 1		Planning		Critical Thinking	Drama 1	Drama 1
Teacher 19	Fine Arts				Eurethmics	Band I, II, III	Planning	Music Appreciation
Teacher 20	Career and Tech.	Food Prep, Nutrition, & Wellness		Dance Tech I, II, III	Planning	Critical Thinking	Food Prep, Nutrition, & Wellness	Dance Tech I, II, III

Potential Barriers

Implementing reading interventions within secondary school settings is critical and challenging. Recent research highlights specific challenges, including a lack of understanding among instructional personnel regarding the need for and expected results of intervention programs, limited empirically validated intervention strategies for higher-level reading skills, and few valid, reliable, and sufficiently sensitive tools to monitor intervention effectiveness, in addition to a variety of organizational barriers related to staff development, scheduling, and funding (Sansosti, Telzrow, & Noltemeyer, 2010).

Staff Development. The need to provide school personnel with professional development to improve their skills and knowledge in regards to working within an RTI framework is well documented and is, in fact, the most often-cited factor related to effective RTI implementation (Harlacher & Siler, 2011). Professional development topics should include the *why* of RTI, including what RTI is, what it takes to implement the framework, and what the expected results are, as well as topics such as high-quality instructional practices, the problem-solving process, assessment, and data-informed instruction. Professional development should be provided on an ongoing basis and include job-embedded learning opportunities and coaching whenever possible (Batsche, Curtis, Dorman, Castillo, & Porter, 2007). Providing teachers with time to collaborate and problem solve student literacy problems and to receive follow-up coaching and feedback is equally essential (National High School Center, National Center on Response to Intervention, and Center on Instruction, 2010).

Scheduling. Although no easy feat, schools must develop master schedules that are flexible enough to allow for extended learning for students who require additional support along with options for students who do not. In addition to this challenge, schools should also attempt to provide instructional personnel with scheduled time for analyzing data and planning and monitoring instruction and interventions. In our experience, improvement in student outcomes (literacy or otherwise) is dependent on the commitment of schools and districts to set aside resources that allow for regular and frequent staff collaboration and for the scheduling of intervention time into the school day. Even when schools have the best of intentions, interventions for students are unlikely to be effective in the absence of time for collaborative problem solving and directed, readily available interventions.

Resources. Challenges associated with accessing adequate intervention, personnel, assessment, and time resources are commonly cited as a barrier for RTI implementation (National High School Center, National Center on Response to Intervention, and Center on Instruction, 2010). Because of many competing initiatives, secondary school personnel may feel overwhelmed and pulled in many directions. Given these often legitimate feelings and circumstances, we have found it is essential for teams to determine ways to work *smarter* rather than *harder.* As a result, our initial work with a school often involves understanding the school's team/meeting structures, current intervention practices, and assessment tools and protocols. An examination of these infrastructure pieces often reveals the existence of multiple school teams that significantly overlap or are not aligned with the school's goals, have ineffective intervention programs, and waste time overassessing students. When duplicated teams are integrated and misaligned teams are eliminated, the meeting time and personnel energy can be redirected to better support the school's literacy goals.

Although common practice, asking school staff to do more without reducing their activity/responsibility in another area is unreasonable. This practice leads to poorly implemented programs and overly taxed personnel. Instead, leadership teams should review all existing intervention practices to determine duplication of services and to identify ineffective instructional/ intervention strategies and programs. Eliminating duplication of services (i.e., multiple people providing the same intervention/support) and stopping ineffective instructional/intervention strategies or programs frees up time, personnel, and other resources needed to implement more effective instructional/intervention programs.

Finally, as discussed throughout this book, working to align and integrate existing intervention programs with core instruction ensures that schools get the most out of their existing intervention resources. We have found that designing effective intervention programming is less about securing additional resources and more related to being strategic about how existing resources are utilized to meet the school's goals.

Fidelity. Student response to intervention and thus intervention effectiveness is impossible to evaluate if interventions are not implemented as they were intended to be, or in other words, with fidelity. Specific factors have been found to negatively impact the fidelity of intervention/implementation, including highly complex or difficult to implement intervention components, required materials that are not readily available to interventionists, interventionists' perceptions that an intervention lacks current or potential effectiveness, and a large number of interventionists with high levels of expertise required for implementation (Johnson, Mellard, Fuchs, & McKnight, 2006).

We have found that providing interventionists with explicit training, follow-up coaching support, and high quality feedback significantly increases the likelihood of intervention fidelity. Along these lines, Gunn recommends the following training, coaching, and resources to support interventionists' intervention implementation (as cited in Protheroe, 2008, p. 40):

- ◆ Learning of the program—both curriculum content and approaches for instructional delivery, including ways to provide explicit instruction, demonstrate skills and strategies, guide student practice, and provide corrective feedback
- ◆ Staff observation of the practice in operation—either by visiting other schools or classrooms or by allowing teachers time to practice and observe one another during initial implementation
- ◆ Teaching time during which teachers develop comfort and fluency and assess how the approach works with their students
- ◆ Observation by other staff members who have been trained in what they should be observing, with feedback provided as a way to increase fidelity of implementation, not as an evaluation of teaching quality in general
- ◆ Refinement through teacher use of observation feedback, grade-level or team meetings to discuss the practice and its implementation, and development of some "calibration checks" for teachers to use to monitor their own implementation

Conclusion

A substantial number of students arrive in secondary schools with below-level literacy skills. The absence of grade-level literacy skills places the students at significant risk for course failures and high school dropout. Without intensive intervention, a large percentage of nonproficient readers leave high school without a diploma and become adults who are less likely to be employed and more likely than high school graduates to live below the poverty line.

Fortunately, much can be done to close skill gaps and improve students' comprehension of grade-level text. These improvements result in higher levels of student success within their courses and higher graduation rates. However, to accomplish these goals, schools and districts must choose to intervene with students before they fail courses, utilize student diagnostic data to inform intervention programming, develop a master schedule that allows for staff collaboration and intervention during the school day, and regularly collect and review data to evaluate the effectiveness of intervention programs.

Although critical, this shift will not be easy, because it requires schools and districts to make difficult decisions related to their current methods of identifying at-risk students, allocating resources, and serving below-level readers. With this in mind, we encourage schools and districts to start small, for example, by focusing on initially implementing an RTI framework to support students as they transition between school levels (typically sixth and ninth grade). Once the school experiences some success within the critical transition years and buy-in and school personnel skills develop (e.g., problem solving, data analysis, intervention design), the RTI framework can be scaled up to support students in upper grades.

7

Teacher Support

Efforts to improve student achievement can succeed only by building the capacity of teachers to improve their instructional practice and the capacity of school systems to advance teacher learning.

—Wei, Darling-Hammond, Andree,
Richardson, & Orphanos, S., 2009

It should come as no surprise at this point in the book that we ardently believe that no action plan is complete without addressing teacher support through professional development and instructional coaching. Research on the amount of time teachers spend participating in professional development indicates that teachers at successful schools meet on a monthly or weekly basis, while teachers at unsuccessful schools meet a few times a year or never. Teachers at gap-closing schools participate in professional development clearly focused on "linking data on low-performing students with effective instructional strategies" (Oberman & Symonds, 2005, p. 10). The connection between providing teachers with high-quality professional development and support designed to link ongoing progress monitoring of student needs to dynamic instructional changes is clear. Thus, guiding and supporting teachers to implement effective instructional strategies to improve student achievement is an essential element of all action plans.

Many schools attempt to "teacher proof" reading intervention by purchasing programs "guaranteed" to improve student literacy achievement. However, current research on reading intervention programs indicates most of these programs are insufficient to meet the needs of all learners (What Works Clearing House, 2011). Instead, schools need to provide teachers with professional development and support to enable them to improve instructional practice and provide precise interventions specific to student needs. Fisher and Frey (2007) argue for precision in teaching that can be realized only "when teachers have an extensive knowledge base and make expert decisions, based on data, about the instructional needs of their students" (p. 32). Developing an action plan to address students' needs through a well-defined multitiered support system will not result in improved student achievement unless a plan to provide teachers with the professional development and instructional coaching they need to implement the desired changes is also developed and implemented.

We begin by determining the instructional needs of students and then identifying professional development barriers to implementing the strategies required to meet their needs. These professional development barriers serve as the basis for the planning of the professional development opportunities that will allow teachers to make the instructional changes necessary to meet student literacy goals. A successful professional development plan provides for "high-quality, sustained professional learning throughout the school year, at every grade level and in every subject" (Wei, Darling-Hammond, Andree, Richardson, & Orphanos, 2009, p. ii). As with student achievement, teacher support must be carefully designed based on student and teacher data and provided through a multitiered system.

The National Staff Development Council (2001) (recently renamed Learning Forward) identified standards for staff development that have been adopted and/or modified by 40 states. These standards provide guidance to schools for designing effective staff development action plans focused on context standards, process standards, and content standards (see Figure 7.1). These standards align closely to our concept of developing action plans utilizing the problem-solving process based on careful analysis of student data. Just as with students, the professional development plan is modified as the effectiveness of the professional development and its impact on instructional changes is monitored. We suggest schools plan for professional development that includes formal professional development followed by ongoing support through job-embedded coaching and deliberate practice opportunities (e.g., professional learning communities and instructional coaching).

Formal Professional Development

Traditional professional development in the United States centers on the workshop model. Under this model, teachers attend sessions facilitated by professional developers who provide instruction on a specific topic. Generally, these occur outside the school instructional day. Many schools and districts provide formal professional development over the summer, on early-release days, after school, on Saturdays, or during "pre-school" days when teachers are preparing for students. In some schools and districts, teachers

FIGURE 7.1 NSDC's Standards for Staff Development

NSDC's Standards for Staff Development

Context Standards

Staff development that improves the learning of all students

- Organizes adults into learning communities whose goals are aligned with those of the school and district (Learning Communities)
- Requires skillful school and district leaders who guide continuous instructional improvement (Leadership)
- Requires resources to support adult learning and collaboration (Resources)

Process Standards

Staff development that improves the learning of all students

- Uses disaggregated student data to determine adult learning priorities, monitor progress, and help sustain continuous improvement (Data-Driven)
- Uses multiple sources of information to guide improvement and demonstrate its impact (Evaluation)
- Prepares educators to apply research to decision making (Research-Based)
- Uses learning strategies appropriate to the intended goal (Design)
- Applies knowledge about human learning and change (Learning)
- Provides educators with the knowledge and skills to collaborate (Collaboration)

Content Standards

Staff development that improves the learning of all students

- Prepares educators to understand and appreciate all students, create safe, orderly and supportive learning environments, and hold high expectations for their academic achievement (Equity)
- Deepens educators' content knowledge, provides them with research-based instructional strategies to assist students in meeting rigorous academic standards, and prepares them to use various types of classroom assessments appropriately (Quality Teaching)
- Provides educators with knowledge and skills to involve families and other stakeholders appropriately (Family Involvement)

are allowed to attend off-site professional development provided through institutes, conferences, or educational organizations. The problem with this type of professional development is that it is infrequently followed by ongoing support and coaching, which translates into limited instructional changes and minimal impact on student achievement.

However, with clearly defined ongoing support, formalized professional development can be an effective tool for instituting instructional changes. The idea is to identify specific professional needs of teachers and develop a long-term professional development plan. This plan may begin with a formal presentation provided by an expert as long as the plan includes opportunities for continued teacher support through professional learning communities and instructional coaching.

Effective formalized professional development focuses on preparing teachers to develop clearly defined pedagogical skills and to provide instruction that meets individual student needs within the content area (Wei, Darling-Hammond, Andree, Richardson, & Orphanos, 2009). All professional development needs to be targeted to provide teachers with the support they need to help students reach school-wide achievement goals.

Professional Learning Communities

Professional learning communities (PLCs) can serve as the first level of ongoing support for previously provided formalized professional development. Recognizing that professional development is most effective "when teachers engage actively in instructional inquiry in the context of collaborative professional communities, focused on instructional improvement and student achievement" (Wei et al., 2009, p. 59), many schools establish PLCs as a means to provide time for teachers to engage in collaborative inquiry focused on improving student achievement. It's important that schools set clearly defined goals related to improving teaching and learning and then allow teachers time for reflection, collaboration, and planning.

Occasionally, schools require teachers to meet in PLCs and provide time within the school calendar for the meetings. However, the schools are often remiss in setting a purpose for the PLCs and setting clear expectations for the expected outcomes of PLC meetings. As a result, PLC meetings often evolve into teacher venting sessions and are often considered a waste of time by all involved. Implementing PLCs requires more than just setting aside time and telling teachers to meet and plan.

In the beginning, facilitators can help guide the discussions and keep the learning community focused on improving teaching and learning (Fisher &

Frey, 2007). Facilitators are key to ensuring the PLC engages in the problem-solving process as a means of making informed decisions. They are useful in helping organize the PLC and keeping it focused on the expected outcomes. Facilitators also can help guide the conversations to allow for inclusion of all members' ideas and concerns.

Ensuring the success of the PLC is largely dependent upon the group dynamics and established protocols. Successful teams establish protocols, embrace diversity, maintain focus on student learning, and engage in ongoing dialogue. The following guidelines are useful for organizing the PLC and ensuring its success.

Developing PLC Norms. Creating an environment that allows for collaborative participation of all parties is paramount for ensuring that all members of the PLC have an equal voice in planning and implementing changes. Therefore, identifying norms should be one of the goals of the first meeting. Some suggestions for team norms that help ensure that all members have a voice in the change process include the following:

- ◆ Respect the input of all members
- ◆ Listen to one another and speak one at a time
- ◆ Disagree agreeably
- ◆ Share air time
- ◆ Accept and respect each person's knowledge base
- ◆ Keep sidebar conversations to a minimum
- ◆ Stay focused on the problem/issue at hand

Embracing Diversity. Recognizing that change is difficult, it's important to take time to ensure PLCs comprise diverse members who bring with them their own perspectives and background experiences (Fullan, 1999). Establishing PLCs that include teachers with varied perspectives encourages resistant teachers to consider new ideas. Oftentimes, it is the lone voice that allows for insight into alternative solutions that might otherwise be missed. Facilitators can help PLCs view "difference as a resource rather than a liability" (Grossman, Wineburg, & Woolworth, 2001, p. 991) and guide the PLC to allow for and encourage alternative viewpoints. The result is to provide all stakeholders with the opportunity to have an active voice in the change process, leading to stronger implementation of changes necessary to achieve school-wide goals.

Maintaining Focus. Successful PLCs maintain their focus on student learning throughout the year. Recognizing that diverse members may, in fact, have diverse agendas, PLCs must maintain their focus on student learning in order to ensure success. DuFour (2004, p. 11) argues that professional learning communities are successful when they "focus on learning rather than teaching, work collaboratively, and hold [themselves] accountable for results." Shifting the focus from teaching to learning allows the PLC to think about what students are doing instead of criticizing one another for what they are or are not doing. In order to achieve these goals, PLCs need to focus on collecting student data, researching appropriate interventions to improve student achievement, setting student achievement goals, and continuing to monitor student progress throughout the year to determine whether or not the plans are successful.

Equally important is the need for PLCs to focus on clearly defined goals. For PLCs to be successful, they must "have real work to do and real decisions to make" (Lyons & Pinnell, 2001, p. 19). PLCs must take care to avoid having regularly scheduled meetings where information is delivered, but no real purpose is achieved. When this occurs, meetings tend to turn into gripe sessions or deteriorate into discussions of school-related issues separate from the PLC's mission. Well-trained facilitators are useful in helping PLCs concentrate on the ultimate goal of improving student learning, providing team members with a clearly focused reason to participate in the process that goes well beyond simply receiving information (Birchak et al., 1998).

Engaging in Ongoing Dialogue. Encouraging dialogue within the PLC ensures that all voices and consequently innovative and creative ideas are heard. Creating a safe, trusting environment where all members participate in ongoing dialogue as a means of addressing complex issues is essential. In dialogue, members of PLCs present different views as a way of discovering new perspectives and freely and creatively explore complex, subtle issues. Dialogue allows for active listening to occur, which requires members to suspend their own views as they listen to the views of others, resulting in deeper understanding of the issues at hand. Dialogue allows for community building and the examination of ideas without judgment (Garmston & Wellman, 1998) and involves the process of gathering and sharing information rather than debating an opinion. Grossman, Wineburg, & Woolworth (2001) define this as "intellectual midwifery," where team members work together to "assist in the birth of new ideas" (p. 984). Once again, facilitators are helpful in guiding conversations within the PLC to ensure all participants are allowed to engage in the dialogue.

Creating a successful PLC requires time and commitment of all involved parties. Bringing a diverse group of teachers together who are committed to improving student achievement is not an easy task. However, it is a critical component of all successful school improvement efforts.

Instructional Coaching

Effective Coaching. Implementing and sustaining effective instructional changes requires continuous support for teachers who are grappling with infusing the changes into their classrooms. Many schools and districts are adding instructional coaches to their plans as a means of providing ongoing teacher support. We have, however, observed many schools where the role of the instructional coach has become a quasi-administrative role. In these cases, the instructional coach ends up serving the needs of administrators rather than the needs of teachers. Effective coaching demands that a majority of the instructional coach's time be spent working directly with teachers in a collaborative and supportive manner.

The Annenberg Institute for School Reform (2004) suggests effective coaching yields the following benefits:

◆ **Encourages collaborative, reflective practice.** When teachers work with instructional coaches, they tend to "apply their learning more deeply, frequently, and consistently than teachers working alone; teachers improve their capacity to reflect; and teachers apply their learning not only to their work with students but also to their work with each other" (p. 2).

◆ **Promotes positive cultural change.** Coaching helps change the culture of a school or system, thus embedding instructional change within broader efforts to improve school-based culture and conditions (p. 2).

◆ **Encourages the use of data analysis to inform practice.** Coaches can help promote and support instructional changes by focusing on "strategic areas of need that are suggested by evidence rather than by individual and sometimes conflicting opinions" (pp. 3–4).

◆ **Promotes implementation of learning and reciprocal accountability.** A coach's role is to "respond to student and teacher needs in ongoing, consistent, and dedicated ways," which ultimately allows coaches and teachers to "work together and hold each other accountable for improved teaching and learning" (p. 4).

◆ **Supports collective, interconnected leadership across a school system.** Effective coaching supports sustained change by "supporting the goals of effective principals through the coaches by keeping the focus on teaching and learning" (p. 4).

Principals must take care to ensure their coaches are spending a majority of their time (a minimum of 75% of their day) working directly with teachers to support instruction. The value a principal places on protecting a coach's time is directly related to the value teachers place on allowing the coach to work with them.

Intensive Coaching Model. The goal of all professional development plans is to ensure that teachers transfer lessons learned into classroom instruction. For this to occur, teachers need ongoing, job-embedded professional development and support. Professional learning communities provide some support for teachers as they collaborate with their peers to implement instructional changes and discuss outcomes. However, many teachers need additional support through an "intensive coaching model" to meet the demands of the school's literacy plan.

The intensive coaching model provides teachers with intensive support to ensure effective implementation of instructional changes. The model is based on research indicating that instructional coaching, which takes place side by side in the classroom with teachers, is the most effective method for ensuring instructional changes (Diamond, 2006). The intensive coaching model is grounded in the Gradual Release of Responsibility instructional model. Under this model, teachers are provided with direct, explicit instruction followed by modeling and scaffolded support leading to independent practice and mastery (Fisher & Frey, 2008). According to Diamond (2006), the most important roles for coaches are modeling of lessons from a newly selected program, side-by-side coaching as a teacher tries the new program, and collegial feedback to refine implementation. Under the intensive coaching model, teachers receive direct, explicit instruction and modeling through formal professional development opportunities followed by additional instructional coaching support as the coach collaborates with individual classroom teachers to model, co-teach, observe, and debrief within the teacher's classroom. As the teacher's expertise increases, the instructional coach's support decreases.

Not all teachers require support through an intensive coaching model. Some teachers move quickly into implementation after receiving formal professional development. Others can make significant changes in instruction after collaboration with peers through professional learning communities. However, others benefit from working closely with an instructional coach through the intensive coaching model. Hence, as schools develop their professional development support systems, they should include opportunities for teachers to engage in all levels of professional development: formal, PLC, and intensive coaching.

Conclusion

Often, we find that schools tend to neglect teacher support as a vital element of the literacy action plan. Unfortunately, this often results in poor implementation of the plan combined with disgruntled teachers who feel pressured to incorporate changes they neither understand nor embrace. We've often heard principals complain that they don't want to take teachers out of the classroom. However, we argue that the time invested in improving instructional effectiveness is well spent while continuing to engage in ineffective classroom instruction is time wasted. With this in mind, we strongly encourage school teams to include professional development and ongoing support through peer collaboration and instructional coaching within their literacy plans. These additions help support teachers and implementation fidelity and ensure the attainment of the school's literacy goals.

8

Conclusions

We can, whenever we choose, successfully teach ALL children whose school-ing is of interest to us. We already know more than we need to know to do that. Whether or not we do it must finally depend on how we feel about the fact that we haven't so far.

—Ron Edmonds, 1982

As schools transition toward the implementation of Common Core State Stan-dards that specifically identify the literacy standards students must master to meet expectations on state assessments and become college and career ready, it will be critical for schools to focus with laser-like accuracy on improving instruction to adequately prepare students.

Continuous improvement of student literacy outcomes requires a com-mitment of time, personnel resources, and effort devoted to the development and implementation of thoughtfully designed literacy plans. Throughout this book, we have emphasized the elements required for improving student achievement over time. We began with a focus on adolescent literacy and how utilizing the problem solving/response to intervention framework through effective leadership teams can help schools more clearly align instruction with student needs, resulting in improved student achievement. We contin-ued with a discussion focused on essential components to improving student success: student engagement and motivation, effective literacy instruction, implementation of a multitiered system of support, and teacher support. We conclude with a review of the key components necessary for sustainable and ongoing improvement.

As Edmonds (1982) suggests, the choice to implement the necessary changes impacting improving student achievement is ours. We have all the components necessary at our fingertips; the difficulty is in pulling together a united team of committed professionals to engage in the process. Second-ary school personnel must begin to work collaboratively through clearly defined leadership teams to analyze student and school-wide data, define clear goals, identify barriers, develop plans to address the barriers, and utilize data to evaluate the impact and effectiveness of literacy plans. Implementing a problem-solving/response to intervention framework to guide the work of literacy leadership teams (LLTs) allows schools to strategically develop effective plans, collect ongoing progress monitoring to determine the effectiveness of the plan, and modify the plan as needed. Instead of relying on gut instinct and opinion, the teams can utilize the problem-solving process to guide action planning and rely on data to make informed decisions. The ongoing collection of progress-monitoring data and consistently applied program evaluation practices allows LLTs to make timely modifications to the literacy program when necessary and address implementation issues as they arise.

The development of a multitiered system of student supports is critical to LLTs' efforts to address specific student needs and provide sufficient instructional/intervention intensity. We implore schools to begin with an analysis of the effectiveness of core instruction and curriculum. Core instruction and curriculum that does not meet the needs of at least 80% of students should be considered ineffective and augmented to more effectively meet student needs. We caution schools against attempting to intervene their way out of core instruction. Simply adding intervention courses to the master schedule without addressing the weaknesses of the core instructional programming is likely to be unsuccessful. In order for significant, sustainable school improvement to occur, literacy needs must be addressed through cross-content literacy instruction implemented within all core courses.

Given the significant deficits of many secondary students, comprehensive literacy plans likely need to include supplemental (Tier 2) and targeted (Tier 3) literacy supports. Efforts must be made to align Tier 2 and Tier 3 supports with core instructional goals. Participation in Tier 2 and/or Tier 3 intervention programs must result in better outcomes in core courses (e.g., successful course completion). The identification of students in need of supplemental and targeted intervention services is best accomplished through a systematic review of historical data. Students who failed or struggled to meet literacy standards in previous years are likely to experience similar difficulties meeting grade-level standards without intervention support. There is no need to wait for secondary school students to demonstrate literacy deficits by scoring below proficiency standards on state assessments or failing courses. Instead, intervention supports should be provided upon entry into the secondary school setting. Gathering diagnostic data from all identified students allows LLTs to clearly define the students' specific needs. This information should be used to inform intervention planning.

We urge all schools to build capacity within their staff to understand the link between literacy skills and student learning and to view the development of student literacy skills as essential to success within every content area and classroom. Helping educators understand the impact of specific instructional practices, curricular supports, and environmental variables on student literacy outcomes is critical to empowering all educators to devote the time and energy necessary to meet student literacy needs, ensuring effective literacy plan development and implementation. The implementation of high-quality instruction based on research-based instructional practices across the curriculum is critical. Thus, schools must focus not just on what is taught but also on the instructional strategies and curricular and environmental supports required to meet the needs of all students.

Utilizing the problem-solving/response to intervention framework allows LLTs to analyze the effectiveness of instruction based on analysis of student data, to understand the impact of specific instructional, curricular, and environmental changes, and to make necessary changes to core and intervention literacy programs.

The responsibilities of the LLT do not stop after the development of the literacy plan. LLTs must promote all teachers' abilities to identify at-risk students and the barriers to student learning, embed literacy supports and instruction within their lesson plans, engage students in the learning process, and reflect on the effectiveness of instructional strategies and curricular and environmental supports. Teachers will likely require support to learn and utilize a problem-solving process and to successfully implement the specific instructional, curricular, and environmental supports necessary to truly impact student literacy achievement. Thus, LLTs must engage in ongoing support of the literacy plan by supporting teachers to collaboratively utilize a problem-solving protocol through the provision of professional development and coaching. Consequently, all comprehensive literacy plans should include a clearly articulated blueprint for supporting teachers through professional development and instructional coaching that specifically incorporates the type of support to be provided, who specifically provides the support, and timelines for support implementation.

The next steps are yours to take. We do not suggest this is a simple process; rather we suggest that it is a rewarding and worthwhile journey that results in unifying schools into collaborative professional teams clearly focused on improving student literacy achievement. We concur with Ron Edmonds that we can, when we choose, meet the needs of all of students. There are no more capable individuals than our nation's educators to provide students with what they need to be successful in school and in life. Our students' and our nation's futures are dependent on our efforts and expertise as educators.

Works Cited

Afflerbach, P., Pearson, P., & Paris, S. F. (2008). Clarifying differences between reading skills and reading strategies. *The Reading Teacher, 61*, 364–73.

Ainsworth, L. (2003). *Unwrapping the standards: A simpler process to make standards manageable.* Englewood, CO: Lead and Learn Press.

Ainsworth, L. (2003). *Power standards: Identifying the standards that matter the most.* Denver, CO: Advanced Learning Press.

Allington, R. (2009). *What really matters in response to intervention.* Boston, MA: Pearson.

Alvermann, D. (2001). *Effective literacy instruction for adolescents.* Executive summary and paper commissioned by the National Reading Conference. Chicago, IL: National Reading Conference.

Anderman, E., Maehr, M., & Midgley, C. (1999). Declining motivation after the transition to middle school: Schools can make a difference. *Journal of Research and Development in Education, 32*(3), 131–147.

Annenberg Institute for School Reform. (2004). Instructional Coaching. *Professional development strategies that improve instruction.* Retrieved from www.annenberginstitute.org

Archer, A. L. & Hughes, G. A. (2011). *Explicit instruction: Effective and efficient teaching.* New York, NY: Guilford Press.

Batsche, G., Elliott, J., Graden, J. L., Grimes, J., Kovaleski, J. F., Prasse, D., Reschly, D. J., Schrag, J., & Tilly, W. D. (2006). *Response to intervention: Policy considerations and implementation.* Alexandria, VA: National Association of State Directors of Special Education, Inc.

Batsche, G., Curtis, M. J., Dorman, C., Castillo, J. M., & Porter, L. J. (2007). The Florida Problem-Solving/Response to Intervention Model: Implementing a Statewide Initiative. In S. R. Jimerson, M. K. Burns, & A. V. Vanderheyden (Eds.) *Handbook of response to intervention: The science and practice of assessment and intervention* (pp. 378–396). New York, NY: Springer.

Biancarosa, G., & Snow, C. E. (2004). *Reading next—A vision for action and research in middle and high school literacy.* A report to Carnegie Corporation of New York. Washington, DC: Alliance for Excellent Education.

Birchak, B., Connor, C., Crawford, K. M., Kahn, L. H., Kaser, S., Turner, S., & Short, K. G. (1998). *Teacher study groups.* Urbana, IL: National Council of Teachers of English.

Black, P., & Wiliam, D. (1998). Inside the black box: Raising standards through classroom assessment [electronic version]. *Phi Delta Kappan, 80*, 139–148. Retrieved June 10, 2009, from http://www.pdkintl.org/kappan/kbla9810.htm

Bottoms, G. (1998). Improving reading and writing skills in language arts courses and across the curriculum (Research Brief 15). Atlanta, Georgia: Southern Regional Education Board.

Bridgeland, J., Dilulio, J., & Burke Morison, K. (2006). *The silent epidemic: Perspectives of high school dropouts.* Washington, DC: Civic Enterprises.

Bromley, K. (2003). Building a sound writing program. In L. M. Morrow, L. B. Gambrell, & M. Pressley (Eds.), *Best practices in literacy instruction* (2nd ed., pp. 143–165). New York, NY: Guilford Press.

Brozo, W. G. (2010). Response to intervention or responsive instruction? Challenges and possibilities of response to intervention for adolescent literacy. *Journal of Adolescent and Adult Literacy, 53*(4), 277–81.

Cambourne, B. (1995). Toward an educationally relevant theory of literacy learning: Twenty years of inquiry. *Reading Teacher, 49,* 182–192.

Carnegie Council on Advancing Adolescent Literacy. (2010). *Time to act: An agenda for advancing adolescent literacy for college and career success.* New York, NY: Carnegie Corporation of New York.

Christenson, S. L., Reschly, A. L., Appleton, J. J., Berman-Young, S., Spanjers, D. M., & Varro, P. (2008). Best practices in fostering student engagement. In A. Thomas & J. Grimes (Eds.), *Best practices in school psychology V* (pp. 1099–1120). Bethesda, MD: National Association of School Psychologists.

Covey, S. (1989). *The 7 habits of highly effective people.* New York, NY: Simon & Schuster.

Craig, P. (2010). *Reading leadership teams: Collaborative leadership for improving and sustaining student achievement.* Larchmont, NY: Eye On Education.

Craig, P. S. (2006). A descriptive analysis of the relationship between specific teacher characteristics and teacher efficacy in Florida's low-performing public high schools. (Unpublished doctoral dissertation.) University of South Florida, Tampa, FL.

Cunningham, A. E., & Stanovich, K. E. (2003). Reading matters: How reading engagement influences cognition. In J. Flood, D. Lapp, J. Squire, & J. Jensen (Eds.), *Handbook of research on teaching the English language arts* (2nd ed., pp. 666–675). Mahwah, NJ: Lawrence Erlbaum Associates.

Curtis, M. E., & Longo, A. M. (2001, November). Teaching vocabulary to adolescents to improve comprehension. *Reading Online, 5*(4). Retrieved from http://www .readingonline.org/articles/art_index.asp?HREF=curtis/index.html

Darling-Hammond, L. (2002). *Redesigning high schools: What matters and what works.* Stanford, CA: School Redesign Network at Stanford University.

Diamond, L. (2006). *Implementing and sustaining an effective reading program.* Consortium on Reading Excellence. Retrieved from http://www.shastacoe.org/ uploaded/Dept/is/general/Teacher_Section/COREBriefingPaperK-8Reading .pdf

Donovan, M. & Bransford, J. (2005). *How students learn: History, mathematics, and science in the classroom.* Washington, DC: The National Academies Press.

Dreher, S. (2003). A novel idea: Reading aloud in a high school English classroom. *English Journal, 93*(1), pp. 50–53.

DuFour, R. (2004). What is a "professional learning community"? *Educational leadership, 61*(8), 6–11.

DuFour, R., DuFour, R., Eaker, R., & Karhanek, G. (2004). *Whatever it takes: How professional learning communities respond when kids don't learn.* Bloomington, IN: Solution Tree.

Eaker, R., DuFour, R., & DuFour, R. (2002). *Getting started: Reculturing schools to become professional learning communities.* Bloomington, IN: National Educational Service.

Eccles, J. S., Wigfield, A., & Schiefele, U. (1998). Motivation to succeed. In N. Eisenberg (Ed.), *Handbook of child psychology: Volume 3—Social, emotional, and personality development* (5th ed.) (pp. 1017–1095). New York, NY: Wiley.

Edmonds, R. R. (1982). Programs of school improvement: An overview. Paper presented at the National Invitational Conference, Research on Teaching: Implications for Practice (Warrenton, VA, February 25–27, 1982). Retrieved from http://www.eric.ed.gov/PDFS/ED221536.pdf

Fang, Z. & Schleppegrell, M. J. (2010). Disciplinary literacies across content areas: Supporting secondary reading through functional language analysis. *Journal of Adolescent and Adult Literacy, 53*(7), 587–597.

Fenzel, M. L., & O'Brennan, L. M. (2007, April). *Educating at-risk urban African American children: The effects of school climate on motivation and academic achievement.* Paper presented at the annual meeting of the American Educational Research Association, Chicago.

Fisher, D. & Frey, N. (2007). Implementing a schoolwide literacy framework: Improving achievement in an urban elementary school. *The Reading Teacher, 61*(1), 32–43.

Fisher, D. & Frey, N. (2008). *Better learning through structured teaching.* Alexandria, VA: Association for Supervision and Curriculum Development.

Florida Department of Education. (2009). *Florida Assessment for Instruction in Reading: Technical manual, grades 3–1.* Retrieved from http://www.fcrr.org/fair/3-12_Technical_Manual_FINAL.pdf

Florida Department of Education. (2010). Content Focus Reports: Reading. Retrieved from http://fcat.fldoe.org/fccontentfocus.asp.

Fuchs, L. S. & Fuchs, D. (2003). *What is scientifically-based research on progress monitoring?* Washington, DC: National Center on Student Progress Monitoring.

Fuchs L. S., Fuchs, D., and Compton, D. L. (2010). Rethinking response to intervention at middle and high school. *School Psychology Review, 39*, 22–28.

Fullan, M. (1999). *Change forces: The sequel.* Philadelphia, PA: Falmer Press.

Gambrell, L. (1996). Creating classroom cultures that foster reading motivation. *The Reading Teacher, 50*(1), 14–25

Garmston, R. & Wellman, B. (1998). Teacher talk that makes a difference. *Educational Leadership, 55*(7), 30–34.

Gresham, F. M., MacMillan, D. L., Beebe-Frankenberger, M. E., & Bocian, K. M. (2000). Treatment integrity in learning disabilities intervention research: Do we really know how treatments are implemented? *Learning Disabilities Research & Practice, 15*(4), 198–205.

Grossman, P., Wineburg, S., & Woolworth, S. (2001). Toward a theory of teacher community. *Teachers College Record, 103*, 942–1012.

Gutierrez, K.D. (2009). A comprehensive federal literacy agenda: Moving beyond inoculation approaches to literacy policy. *Journal of Literacy Research*, 41: 4. 476–83.

Guthrie, J. T. (2001, March). Contexts for engagement and motivation in reading. *Reading Online, 4*(8). Retrieved from http://www.readingonline.org/articles/handbook/guthrie

Guthrie, J. T., & Humenick, N. M. (2004). Motivating students to read: Evidence for classroom practices that increase reading motivation and achievement. In P. McCardle & V. Chhabra (Eds.), *The voice of evidence in reading research* (pp. 329–54). Baltimore, MD: Paul H. Brookes Publishing.

Guthrie, J. T., Schafer, W. D., & Huang, C. (2001). Benefits of opportunity to read and balanced reading instruction for reading achievement and engagement: A policy analysis of state NAEP in Maryland. *Journal of Educational Research, 94*(3), 145–162.

Guthrie, J. T., & Wigfield, A. (2000). Engagement and motivation in reading. In M. L. Kamil, P. B. Mosenthal, P. D. Pearson, & R. Barr (Eds.), *Handbook of reading research: Volume III* (pp. 403–422). New York, NY: Erlbaum.

Guthrie, J. T., Wigfield, A., Barbosa, P., Perencevich, K. C., Taboada, A., Davis, M. H., Scafiddi, N. T., & Tonks, S. (2004). Increasing reading comprehension and engagement through concept-oriented reading instruction. *Journal of Educational Psychology*, 96 (3). 403–423.

Guthrie, J. T., Wigfield, A., & VonSecker, C. (2000). Effects of integrated instruction on motivation and strategy use in reading. *Journal of Educational Psychology, 92*(2), 331–341.

Hall, B. W., Hines, C. V., Bacon, T. P., & Koulianos, G. M. (1992). Attributions that teachers hold to account for student success and failure and their relationship to teaching level and teacher efficacy beliefs. Paper presented at the annual meeting of the American Educational Research Association, April 19–24, 1992, San Francisco, CA. (ERIC Document Reproduction Service. No. ED349280).

Hammond, C., Linton, D., Smink, J., & Drew, S. (2007). *Dropout risk factors and exemplary programs: A technical manual.* Clemson, SC: National Dropout Prevention Center.

Harlacher, J., & Siler, C. (2011). Factors related to successful RtI implementation. *NASP Communiqué, 39*(6), 20–22.

Harlow, C. (2003). Education and correctional populations. Bureau of Justice Statistics Special Report. Washington, DC: U.S. Department of Justice.

Haselhuhn, C. W., Al-Mabuk, R., Gabriele, A., Groen, M., & Galloway, S. (2007). Promoting positive achievement in the middle school: A look at teachers' motivational knowledge, beliefs, and teaching practices. *Research in Middle Level Education (RMLE Online), 30*(9).

Hattie, J. (2009) *Visible learning: a synthesis of over 800 meta-analyses relating to achievement.* London: Routledge.

Heartland Area Education Agency. (2007). *Heartland special education procedures: Module four, decision making practices.* Retrieved from http://www.aea11.k12.ia .us/spedresources/ModuleFour.pdf

Heller, R. & Greenleaf, C. L. (2007). *Literacy instruction in the content areas: Getting to the core of middle and high school improvement.* Washington, DC: Alliance for Excellent Education.

Heppen, J. B. & Bowles Therriault, S. (2008). Developing early warning systems to identify potential high school dropouts. American Institute for Research. Retrieved from www.betterhighschools.com

Hernandez, D. (2011). Double jeopardy: How third-grade reading skills and poverty influence high school graduation. Baltimore, MD: Annie E. Casey Foundation.

Hogan, K., & Pressley, M. (Eds.). (1997). *Scaffolding student learning: Instructional approaches & issues.* Cambridge, MA: Brookline Books.

Hosp, J. L. (2006, May) Implementing RtI: Assessment practices and response to intervention. *NASP Communiqué*, 34(7). Retrieved from http://www .nasponline.org/publications/cq/cq347rti.aspx

Hosp, J. L. (2008). Best practices in aligning academic assessment with instruction. In A. Thomas & J. Grimes (Eds.), *Best practices in school psychology V* (pp. 363–376). Bethesda, MD: National Association of School Psychologists.

International Reading Association. (2010). *Response to Intervention: Guiding principles for educators from the International Reading Association.* Retrieved from http://www.reading.org/Libraries/Resources/RTI_brochure_web.pdf

Jacobs, V. A. (2008). Adolescent literacy: Putting the crisis in context. *Harvard Educational Review, 78*(1), 7–39.

Johnson, E., Mellard, D. F., Fuchs, D., & McKnight, M. A. (2006). *Responsiveness to intervention (RtI): How to do it.* Lawrence, KS: National Research Center on Learning Disabilities.

Johnstone, C. J.; Thurlow, M. L.; Moen, R. E.; Matchett, D.; Hausmann, K. E.; & Scullin, S. (2007). What do state reading test specifications specify? Partnership for Accessible Reading Assessment. International Center for Special Education Research. Retrieved from http://www.readingassessment.info/resources/publications/PARAblueprintReport.pdf

Kamil, M. L., Borman, G. D., Dole, J., Kral, C. C., Salinger, T., and Torgesen, J. (2008). Improving adolescent literacy: Effective classroom and intervention practices: A practical guide. Washington, DC: National Center for Education Evaluation and Regional Assistance, Institute of Education Sciences, U.S. Department of Education. Retrieved from http://ies.ed.gov/ncee/wwc/pdf/practiceguides/adlit_pg_082608.pdf

Kennelly, L. & Monrad, M. (2007). Easing the transition to high school: Research and best practices designed to support high school learning. Washington, DC: National High School Center.

Kirsch, I.; de Jong, J.; LaFontaine, D.; McQueen, J.; Mendelovits, J.; & Monseur, C. (2002). *Reading for change: Performance and engagement across countries: Results from PISA 2000.* Paris, France: Organization for Economic Co-operation and Development.

Kutner, M., Greenberg, E., Jin, Y., Boyle, B., Hsu, Y., and Dunleavy, E. (2007). Literacy in everyday life: Results from the 2003 National Assessment of Adult Literacy. Washington, DC: National Center for Education Statistics, Institute of Education Sciences, U.S. Department of Education.

Langer, J. A. (2001). Beating the odds: Teaching middle and high school students to read and write well. *American Educational Research Journal, 38*(4), 837–880.

Langer, J. A.; Close, E.; Angelis, J.; & Preller, P. (2000). Guidelines for teaching middle and high school students to read and write well: Six features of effective instruction. Albany, NY: National Research Center on English Learning & Achievement.

Lesnick, J., Goerge, R., Smithgall, C., & Gwynne J. (2010). Reading on grade level in third grade: How is it related to high school performance and college enrollment? Chicago: Chapin Hall at the University of Chicago.

Lyons, C. A. & Pinnell, G. S. (2001). *Systems for change in literacy education.* Portsmouth, NH: Heinemann.

Marks, H. (2000). Student engagement in instructional activity: Patterns in elementary, middle, and high school years. *American Educational Research Journal, 37*(1), 153–184.

Marzano, R. J. (2003). *What works in schools: Translating research into action.* Alexandria, VA: Association for Supervision and Curriculum Development.

Marzano, R. J. (2004) *Building background knowledge for academic achievement: Research on what works in schools.* Alexandria, VA: Association for Supervision and Curriculum Development, 91–103.

Marzano, R. J., Pickering, D. J., & Pollock, J. E. (2001). *Classroom instruction that works: Research-based strategies for increasing student achievement.* Alexandria, VA: Association for Supervision and Curriculum Development.

Mathes, P., Denton, C., Fletcher, J., Anthony, J., Francis, D., & Schatschneider, C. (2005). The effects of theoretically different instruction and student characteristics on the skills of struggling readers. *Reading Research Quarterly, 40*(2), 148–182.

Meltzer, J., Smith, N. C., & Clark, H. (2002). *Adolescent literacy resources: Linking research and practice.* Center for Resource Management. Educational Alliance. Providence, RI: LAB at Brown University.

Miller, T. K. (2002). Using professional standards for program assessment and development. NASPA Net Results.

Moje, E. B. (2008). Foregrounding the disciplines in secondary literacy teaching and learning: A call for change. *Journal of Adolescent and Adult Literacy, 52*(2), 96–107.

Moje, E. B., Overby, M., Tysvaer, N., Morris, K. (2008). The complex world of adolescent literacy: Myths, motivations, and mysteries. *Harvard Educational Review, 78*(1), 107–54.

Morsy, L., Kieffer, M., & Snow, C. E. (2010). *Measure for measure: A critical consumers' guide to reading comprehension assessment for adolescents.* New York, NY: Carnegie Corporation of New York.

Naisbitt, J. & Aburdene, P. (1985). *Reinventing the Corporation.* New York, NY: Warner Books.

National Governors Association Center for Best Practices and the Council of Chief State School Officers. (2010). Common core state standards for English language arts & literacy, history/social studies, science, & technical subjects. Retrieved from http://www.corestandards.org/the-standards

National High School Center, National Center on Response to Intervention, and Center on Instruction. (2010). *Tiered interventions in high schools: Using preliminary "lessons learned" to guide ongoing discussion.* Washington, DC: American Institutes for Research.

National Institute for Literacy. (2007). *What content area teachers should know about adolescent literacy.* Washington, DC: National Institute of Child Health and Human Development.

National Research Council Committee on Increasing High School Students' Motivation to Learn (2003). *Engaging schools: fostering high schools' motivation to learn.* Washington, DC: The National Academies Press.

National Research Council Committee on Increasing High School Students' Engagement and Motivation to Learn. (2004). *Engaging schools.* Washington, DC: The National Academies Press.

National Staff Development Council. (2001). *Standards for staff development (revised).* Oxford, OH: National Staff Development Council.

Newman, F., Marks, H. & Gamoran, A. (1995). Authentic pedagogy and student performance. Conference presentation to the American Educational Research Association. ERIC Document Reproduction Service No. ED 389 679.

No Child Left Behind Act of 2001, 20 U.S.C. § 6319 (2008).

Noe, K. L S. & Johnson, N. J. (1999). *Getting started with literature circles.* Norwood, MA: Christopher-Gordon Publishers, Inc.

Oberman, I. & Symonds, K. W. (2005). What matters most in closing the gap. *Leadership, 34*(3), 8–11.

Parris, S. & Collins Block, C. (2007). The expertise of adolescent literacy teachers. *Journal of Adolescent and Adult Literacy, 50*(7), 582–596.

Pellegrino, J. W., Chudowsky, N., & Glaser, R. (2001). Knowing what students know: The science and design of educational assessment. Washington, DC: National Academy Press.

Pitcher, S. M., Albright, L. K., DeLaney, C. J., Walker, N.T., Seunarinesingh, K., Mogge, S., Headley, K.N., Gentry Ridgeway, V., Peek, S., Hunt, R., Dunston, P.J. (2007). Assessing adolescents' motivation to read. *Journal of Adolescent and Adult Literacy 50*(5): 378–96.

Pressley, M. (2000). What should comprehension instruction be the instruction of? In M. L. Kamil, P. B. Mosenthal, P. D. Pearson, and R. Barr (Eds). *Handbook of reading research, Volume III* (pp. 545–562). Mahwah, NJ: Lawrence Erlbaum.

Pressley, M. (2001). Comprehension instruction: What makes sense now, what might make sense soon. *Reading Online, 5*(2). Retrieved from http://www.readingonline.org

Protheroe, N. (2008, September/October). The impact of fidelity of implementation in effective standards-based instruction. *Principal*, 38–41.

Rebora, A. (April 9, 2010). [Interview with Richard Allington, Professor of Education at the University of Tennessee]. http://www.edweek.org.

Reeves, D. B. (2003). High performance in high poverty schools: 90/90/90 and beyond. Center for Performance Assessment. Retrieved from http://www.sabine.k12.la.us/online/leadershipacademy/high%20performance%2090%2090%2090%20and%20beyond.pdf

Sansosti, F., Telzrow, C. & Noltemeyer, A. (2010). Barriers and facilitators to implementing response to intervention in secondary schools: Qualitative perspectives of school psychologists. *School Psychology Forum, 4*(1), 1–21.

Schmoker, M. (2011). *Focus: Elevating the essentials to radically improve student learning.* Alexandria, VA: Association for Supervision and Curriculum Development.

Shanahan, T. & Shanahan, C. (2008). Teaching disciplinary literacy to adolescents: Rethinking content-area literacy. *Harvard Educational Review, 78*(1), 40–59.

Simmons, D. C., Kameenui, E. J., Stoolmiller, M., Coyne, M. D., & Harn, B. (2003). Accelerating growth and maintaining proficiency: A two-year intervention study of kindergarten and first-grade children at risk for reading difficulties. In B. Foorman (Ed.), Preventing and remediating reading difficulties: Bringing science up to scale, 197–228. Timonium, MD: York Press.

Snow, C. E., & Biancarosa, G. (2003). *Adolescent literacy and the achievement gap: What do we know and where do we go from here?* New York: Carnegie Corporation of New York.

Snow, C. & Moje, E. (2010). Why is everyone talking about adolescent literacy? *Phi Delta Kappan, 91*(6), 66–69.

Stanovich, P. J., & Stanovich, K. E. (2003). Using research and reason in education: How teachers can use scientifically based research to make curricular & instructional decisions. Washington, DC: US Department of Education.

NIFL.pdf. Retrieved from http://www.nifl.gov/partnershipforreading/ publications/html/stanovich/

Strommen, L. T. & Mates, B. F. (2004). Learning to love reading: Interviews with older children and teens. *Journal of Adolescent & Adult Literacy, 48*(3), 188–200.

Thompson, G. L., Warren, S., & Carter, L. (2004). It's not my fault: Predicting high school teachers who blame parents and students for students' low achievement. *High School Journal, 87*(3), 5–14.

Turner, J. C. & Patrick, H. (2004). Motivational influences on student participation in classroom learning activities. *Teachers College Record, 106*(9), 1759–85.

Urdan, T. & Schoenfelder, E. (2006). Classroom effects on student motivation: Goal structures, social relationships, and competence beliefs. *Journal of School Psychology, 44*, 331–349.

UNESCO Institute for Education. (2008). *International literacy statistics: A review of concepts, methodology, and current data.* Retrieved from http://www.uis.unesco .org/template/pdf/Literacy/LiteracyReport2008.pdf

Vacca, R. T. & Vacca, J. A. L. (2008). *Content area reading: Literacy and learning across the curriculum.* Boston, MA: Pearson.

Webb, N. L. (2002). Depth of knowledge levels for four content areas. Retrieved from http://www.providenceschools.org/media/55488/depth%20of %20knowledge%20guide%20for%20all%20subject%20areas.pdf

Wei, R. C., Darling-Hammond, L., Andree, A., Richardson, N., & Orphanos, S. (2009). Professional learning in the learning profession: A status report on teacher development in the United States and abroad. Dallas, TX. National Staff Development Council.

What Works Clearinghouse. (2011). U.S. Department of Education. Institute of Educational Sciences. Retrieved from http://ies.ed.gov/ncee/wwc/reports/ advancedss.aspx

Wiggins, G. & McTighe, J. (2005). *Understanding by design.* Alexandria, VA: Association for Supervision and Curriculum Development.

Wise, B. (2009). Adolescent literacy: The cornerstone of student success. *Journal of Adolescent and Adult Literacy, 52*(5), 369–75.

Worthy, J. (1998). "On every page someone is killed!" Book conversations you don't hear in school. *Journal of Adolescent and Adult Literacy, 41*(7), 508–519.